KING BOB AND HIS BOY JUMBO

This is a work of nonfiction. The events and conversations in this book have been set down to the best of the author's ability, although some names and details may have been changed to protect the privacy of individuals. Every effort has been made to trace or contact all copyright holders. The publishers will be pleased to make good any omissions or rectify any mistakes brought to their attention at the earliest opportunity.

Printed in Australia
Cover design by Shawline Publishing Group Pty Ltd

Printed in Australia

First Printing: Feb 2022

Shawline Publishing Group Pty Ltd
www.shawlinepublishing.com.au

Paperback ISBN-13 9781922594990

Ebook ISBN-13 9781922701121

A catalogue record for this book is available from the National Library of Australia

GEORGE J WATTS

KING BOB AND HIS BOY JUMBO

I dedicate this book to my grandchildren and great-grandchildren who never had the chance to know and understand their grandfather.

EARLY YEARS

*

King Bob, King of the bottleos, was my Dad. He earned his living collecting beer bottles and scrap iron. As a baby, I spent the first part of my life in a wooden box on my Dad's bottle cart. It was in 1931, at the height of the Great Depression. As I got older, Dad told me stories of how he carried me in a pineapple box to different hotels to find a mother breastfeeding her baby. For a little money, they were more than willing to see that I didn't go hungry. Nearly every hotel in Fitzroy and Collingwood had a concrete horse trough full of water outside the hotel. It was the owner of the hotel's way of attracting a customer. When I dirtied myself, the horse trough was my bath. Dad washed me then put me in a clean box. I was soon known as The Pineapple Kid and the name stuck to me for several years until one day Dad decided to call me Jumbo. Many a day I spent my time on the cart in a wooden box while Dad worked the back lanes of Collingwood collecting beer bottles or scrap iron. If not, one of dad's ladies looked after me. Years later, I went out of my way to find these mothers who by now were in the twilight of their lives, with some success.

MY BIRTH

*

It was my Grandma who told me how I came into this world. Grandma said, "Your Dad came home in one of his nasty moods and gave your mother a beating, then went out again, leaving her on the floor. She was too frightened to tell anyone. It was the beating that caused you to be born premature. If I hadn't called in to see your mother, who was all alone with your four young brothers and sisters, you may not be here today. When I arrived at the house, she was in a bad way. Your Dad came home later that evening with his drunken mates and I thought there was going to be a fight, so I locked the children in the back bedroom." Grandma said I was born around midnight. My Dad said it was before. No one was too sure as there was no clock in the house. For the next forty years I celebrated my birthday on the 6. 2. 1931 until I needed my birth certificate and it said I was born on the 7. 2.1931

CAST OFF

*

I arrived into this world amongst drunken people. Drunkenness was to be a part of my life for the next twelve years. I try to imagine the scene the night I came into this world. Dad in the kitchen with his mates, beer bottles scattered on the kitchen table, he too drunk to worry about his wife, who was just about to give birth. Little did he realise, or did he and maybe that is why he hit my mother earlier in the day, that Dick his best mate, a tall, dark and rather good-looking guy who was in the kitchen, had more than a passing interest in the colour of the baby's hair.

I was five weeks old when my mother decided I was not her boyfriend's baby. This proved correct. The colour of my hair was the same as the rest of my brothers and sisters. This had a lot to do with why my mother decided to abandon me. My mother had three more children and they were all dark- headed, like her boyfriend. At least I was not born a bastard. This affair caused the family to split up. Grandma took in my eldest brother Bob, eight years old and my sister June, five years. My mother kept Jack, seven, and Shirley, three years old. No one wanted me. Dad decided to keep me, for what reason only he knew. The impact it left on our lives was never repaired. It was as if we were three different families. The older ones had nothing to do with the younger ones. The family wanted nothing to do with Dad and their baby brother. In later years, some emerged out of their burrows, seeking to make contact, but it was all too late. There were too many time gaps to be filled.

MY DAD

*

Dad came into this world in 1903. His motto was, "You can't live more than a day at a time." Materialism didn't mean a thing to him. His deeds as a bottleo were known far and wide amongst the rag and bone men. Others would boast to their mates, "I worked with the King today." He could pull a load of bottles where others failed. He was known as King Bob. He was my Dad, and as a young boy I believed whatever he said was right. As the years pass by, I can see him now, in his bib and brace overalls long overdue for the rag bag. A shoulder strap hung loosely; the buckle had lost its battle with the rusty nail long ago. His shirt-sleeves firmly rolled up around his wiry muscles as he walked towards me, carrying a bag of bottles on his back. I would jump down from the cart with two bent nails ready for Dad to fasten the top of the bag before the bottles spilled over the floor of the cart.

His hard life was revealed in his face, weather-beaten with deep lines across his forehead. He was bald except for a tuft of floating, fine hair. He was also without teeth for as long as I can remember. One of his favorite sayings was, "It's better to be without teeth than to have them knocked out in a fight!" Many a time, I witnessed a beating or a victory in a street fight when Dad had too much to drink. Yet when he was sober, he possessed a charm that drew people to him, especially women who lounged around the hotels looking for an easy drink. I was so proud of my Dad. He could do no wrong. Dad had few memories of his own father who'd deserted the family when he was a toddler, leaving my grandmother barely surviving in an old, dilapidated farmhouse. Life would not have been easy for my Gran, with three young children to bring up on her own. There was no point going to the mailbox for a Social Services cheque. It didn't exist. Grandma had to rely on charity and friends. Dad said he remembered his mother was given a cow and she said it came from heaven, and if they took care of it, God wouldn't take it away. Dad said he didn't understand, as he had never met God. It must have been hard for a seven-year-old boy to be given the job of milking the cow.

Dad had to get up early and look for the cow in the thick scrub, then bring it back to the tin shed and do the milking before he went to school. His mother's sewing machine never stopped making clothes for the rich people. It was her way of making a little money to survive.

One morning, Dad's little sister wandered away from the house. My dad said, "Little Maude was found floating face down in a dam about a mile from the house." With a young family to take care of and a failed marriage, Grandma decided to make a new life for herself and her two boys and moved to Melbourne. She rented a two-story house in Gore Street, Fitzroy and took in boarders to help make ends meet. This was to be her home for the next sixty-seven years. I have often wondered if my Grandma had stayed in Creswick, would my father have been any different.

As for my mother, she came from a very large family. Her father made his living collecting beer bottles. If there was ever such a thing as an honest bottleo, he was one of them. My grandfather was one of the few bottleos that had a regular round of customers. Sometimes, I would see him in Johnson Street, Collingwood, sitting in his covered wagon, chewing dark plugged tobacco and talking to the knife sharpener, who was sitting on his bike pedaling away as he sharpened someone's knife on the sandstone wheel. Every now and again, the knife man poured water over the sandstone, then pedaled a little faster, moving the knife sideways. If Dad wasn't around, I'd stop and talk to my grandfather. He would often say, "Come on Jumbo, come and work with me," knowing all the time I'd say no.

My mother's brothers were so different from Granddad. They either spent time in jail, or paid fines for stealing. They never gave it a second thought to walking into a backyard and taking the empty bottles if they knew no one was home. Dad met my mother at a football match. That fatal day was to change his life forever. He left his apprenticeship as an electro-plater and started working on the bottle cart with my mother's brothers and joined them in their drinking sprees. My Grandma told me my Dad never put a drop of liquor to his mouth before he became acquainted with that family.

FIRST DAY AT SCHOOL

*

I was seven years old before I saw the inside of a school. When Dad decided to have a break from drinking, he had this saying, maybe it was a feeling of guilt. "Jumbo, you are going to start school." The next morning, Dad gave me a shilling to buy my lunch. I didn't want to go to school. I wanted to be with my dad. At that time, we lived in Marine Parade, just a short walk to St Heliers school Abbotsford. Just before school time, I decided to hang around the street corner a short distance from the school. I heard the bell ring and then waited for the kids to disappear. Pleased with myself for not going to school, I was not too sure what I wanted to do. I decided to spend the day under the bluestone bridge that crossed the Yarra River, at the bottom end of Johnson Street. It was one of my favourite places, catching minnows trapped between the rocks until it was time to see Dad. He never seemed to get upset when I said I didn't go to school and had spent the day playing down at the river. He would growl a little and say, "I will take you to school tomorrow," which never happened.

THE MAN IN THE GREY SUIT

*

A few days later, we were just about to leave for work when a man in a grey suit came through the back gate. He was tall and mean-looking, his grey felt hat with a coloured feather, slightly tilted to one side. He asked Dad was he Mr. Watts. My Dad told me to go inside while they talked. I went to my bedroom, and from my window I could see the man waving his hands in the air as he walked away. Then I heard Dad swear in a loud voice and called out to me, "Jumbo, that man is captain of the John Murray. He wants to know if there are any boys here that are not going to school". Those few words frightened the hell out of me. There were other days Dad threatened me when I was in his bad books. Dad would say, "I will put you on the John Murray." It was a ship that came to Melbourne and took naughty boys away and they never came back. In later years, I came to realise the John Murray never existed. It was one of Dad's made-up stories. "Jumbo, tomorrow you are going to start school or the man is coming back to take you away." The next morning, I was still in bed when Dad called out, "Jumbo, are you ready for school?" Again, I didn't want to go, I wanted to be with my Dad. As I left the house with just my lunch money, Dad threatened me again, "If you don't go to school that man will come back." I promised Dad to come to the pub after school.

I BURNT THE TREE DOWN

*

On my way to school, I had to pass our local milk bar. Outside the shop was a gum tree with a big hollow hole at the bottom of its trunk, I decided to wait next to the tree until the school bell rang then I went into the shop and bought a box of Redhead matches with two pennies from my lunch money. While I was waiting for the last of the school kids to disappear, I kept looking at the big hole and the dry leaves with one thought in mind, to set fire to the tree. I gathered up a few dry leaves and lit a fire. The flames raced up the hollow trunk. The tree was smoking as if it had three chimneys. I hurried away from the burning tree, with no thought of going to school. I went back to the bottle yard and waited for my Dad. It was too early; Dad wouldn't be back until lunchtime.

BARNEY

*

Barney, the owner of the bottle yard always wore a long leather apron with a large pocket where he kept his money in a small bag to pay the bottleos for their bottles and whatever else they had to sell, like scrap metal, rags or anything else of value. Just about every day, ten to twelve bottleos came into the yard to sell their bottles using many different types of horse-drawn carts such as covered wagons or a two-wheel cart with a tip tray or lorries. Those who couldn't afford the money to hire a horse and cart for the day pulled a two-wheel cart around the streets close to the bottle yard, hoping to collect bottles. After selling their bottles some bottleos made straight for their drinking hole, others went home to their families, more than satisfied with their day's work. At the back of the bottle yard was a large tin shed where there were several large iron tubs full of bottles in hot soapy water, using their last bit of air to keep afloat. Fixed across the hot tubs were several spinning scratch brushes for the men to wash the inside of bottles. Then they were passed on to the next trough and rinsed in warm water. There were rows of different washed bottles stacked against the shed wall, plain wine bottles, sauce bottles, and many other different brands ready to be packed and sent away. Barney was used to me hanging around the yard. Many times, I helped him sort the plain bottles from the branded ones and stacked the beer bottles in the wooden crates, ready to be loaded onto the brewery truck. Barney's bottle yard was at the far end of Little Charles Street in Abbotsford. The cobbled bluestone laneway was barely wide enough for two carts to pass. I was waiting for my Dad at the bottle yard double gates when his horse and cart appeared at the end of the lane. I knew it was my Dad by the load of bottles stacked high. The sight of seeing Dad made me run as fast as my legs could carry me. He didn't seem a bit surprised to see me as I climbed onto the cart amongst the bags of bottles. Dad didn't say a word about school. I knew he was pleased to see me. There was a big smile on his face when he saw there were no other bottleo's carts in the yard. My Dad always liked to be first back with the biggest load of bottles. When we finished unloading, Barney came with his pad and counted the bottles, and paid Dad his money, except seven and sixpence for the hire of the horse and cart.

I was waiting for my Dad to say something about me not going to school. "What happened Jumbo?" "Dad, I burnt a tree; I don't want to go to school." My Dad didn't growl or threaten me with the John Murray. When we got back to the hotel, Dad started telling his mates how I burnt the tree down; he was having a great laugh with his mates. I knew I was not in trouble and wouldn't be sent away on the John Murray. For the rest of the afternoon, Dad played cards until the pub closed.

A few days later, somehow the man in the tilted hat found out where Dad sold his bottles. One morning, he was waiting for us when we drove into the yard. I really thought I was a goner. I ran out of the bottle yard and waited for Dad at the pub. The next morning, Dad decided to take me to school himself. He said I could drive the horse and cart to school if I behaved myself. I liked nothing better than to hold the reins. As I approached the school, the kids were looking at me. I gave the horse a flap on the rump with the reins. I was now the centre of attention and loving every bit of it. I jumped down from the cart and waved as Dad drove away. Clutching the lunch money Dad had given me, suddenly I felt all alone. The school kids were still staring at me. I had this feeling I didn't belong there. Then the school bell rang and all the kids ran towards an area, lined up and went inside. I waited for the kids to disappear to their classrooms before walking slowly towards a set of brick steps, thinking about the John Murray. I hesitated for a moment, thinking for sure Dad was going to send me away this time if I didn't go through those big wooden double doors that kept staring at me. I was not too sure where I should go but I could hear children singing.

A MONSTER STRUCK ME TWICE

*

Suddenly, a door opened. I was taken by surprise. A monster appeared in a black hood and white bib. It towered right over me. As I looked up at her face, a voice said, "What is your name little boy and what are you doing here?" I mumbled something about Dad sending me to school and that I was lost. I was not too sure what was going to happen. I followed her to another room where another monster was sitting at a huge desk, which seemed to take up most of the room. I looked around the room and felt I was being swallowed up by a thousand books. "What is your name and where do you live? Are you the boy who burnt down the tree?" asked the monster sitting behind the desk. I was too scared to say no. I was sure they had seen me do it. I was told to face the corner while they talked in soft voices.

I tried to listen but couldn't understand a word. I was then taken along a narrow pathway to a large building. It was a church, the same one that overlooked the high grey cement wall that ran from one end of the street to the other. The large wooden door was open. As we entered the church and passed rows of wooden pews, I looked up at the ceiling; it seemed so high to me. All the glass windows were covered in a mass of paintings. I could see faces and bright colours. After what seemed like a long walk, we came to a classroom full of kids. They looked big, sitting in their desks. The monster said, "This is the boy who burnt the tree down. He is going to be punished for destroying such a beautiful tree." I was told to kneel down in front of the class and hold out both my hands. From my kneeling position, the monster looked twice as big. I remember looking at her shiny black shoes with large silver buckles. As I looked up, my eyes met hers. The look of hatred made me turn away as she drew the strap over her shoulder. The monster struck me twice. I did not cry. I was a pretty determined kid for my age. I then had to stand on a raised, wooden platform and was told to say, "I am sorry for burning down the tree." This I had to repeat until I said it properly.

Then I was taken to another classroom where children were standing on their desk seats singing a Jesus song. I was greeted by someone else wearing a long white something with a sort of hat, which looked different. She gave me a smile and asked me my name. I wouldn't answer. I guess she knew what I had just been through. A card with a picture of a lady was put in my hand. I was starting to feel sick. Everyone was singing, "Jesus loves me, yes I know, for the Bible tells me so." Suddenly I made a dash for the door, leaving a trail of vomit behind. As usual, I went to the bottle yard and waited for Dad. I told him I got the strap for burning the tree down. There were times my Dad said to me, "I can teach you more about how to survive in life working the bottle cart than going to school." That was my first and last day at school for several weeks.

ON THE CART

*

Next to the bottle yard were the horse stables. I was good at helping. While Dad was putting the harness on Dobby's back, I'd hitch the leather traces to the cart, then search the ground for nails to fasten the bags of bottles we would collect later on. As Dad drove away from the bottle yard, his right leg dangled over the side of the cart, and his left was firmly fixed on the draw carriage to support himself. Dad liked holding the reins loosely in one hand.

Occasionally, he gave Dobby a flap on the rump to keep her mind on the job.

One morning we were having fried bread and dripping for breakfast. Dad said,

"Dripping is good for greasing your bones." It was his way of making an excuse for having no food in the house. "Today, I think we'll work around Kew Junction. We could try the laneway behind the shops where we saw the bath heaters." Hearing those few words, I was excited at the thought of Dad making money. Dobby trotting along Johnson Street at a steady pace took about twenty minutes before we pulled up in the lane. My Dad told me to grab a sack bag and work the short lane on the other side of the street while he went after the bath heaters. I was nearly eight years of age and knew how to pick up a sack bag and throw it over my shoulder, just like my Dad. Walking towards the lane, my mind was full of hope. I might get a bag of rags, or a battery or two. I could hear Dad arguing with the woman, up to his old tricks, telling the lady the heaters were burnt out and he was doing her a favour by taking them away. His motto was, "If you can avoid it, never pay for anything, but if they insist, put a little money in their hand." I collected my share of bottles, more than once returning to the cart with another bag half full. At one stage, I was going to pass a couple of houses, thinking it was a waste of time. Then remembered what my Dad had taught me, "Never pass a gate without having a look first. It just might be the call that makes your day." With these powerful thoughts in mind, I retraced my steps. The first backyard had nothing of interest, just a few beer bottles stacked against the tin fence. Next to the tin gate was a shed. My eye followed the rusty chain through the small hole and to my delight I saw a double brass bed leaning up against the shed wall.

I went to no end of trouble to make myself heard. I banged and kicked the double gate for several minutes, but to no avail. The thought of leaving the bed behind made me knock again. Then a lady opened the tin gate, wanting to know what all the noise was. I said I was collecting bottles and did she want to sell the ones against the fence. I did what my Dad had taught me, "If you ever see something good, take no notice of it at first." So, I bagged up the few bottles - I had some money in my hand - and just when I was about to pay for the bottles, I looked her straight in the eye and said, "Do you want to get rid of the old bed in the shed?"

The bed was covered in brass and I bought it for three shillings, but it was too heavy for me to carry back to the cart. The lady helped me to rest it against the tin fence. Then I went and got my Dad, who had a big smile on his face as he carried the brass bed back to the cart. I was pleased with my efforts; I knew the scrap brass was worth at least one pound. It wasn't long before we had a full load and it was still early. This meant we had plenty of time to be first back to the bottle yard. I felt proud sitting on top of the bags of bottles as we made our way back. Dad didn't say a word about the bed. I knew he was pleased with me. It was about eleven thirty when we arrived at the bottle yard. This pleased my Dad. There were the usual wine dots waiting to help Dad unload the cart. They all knew Dad was more than generous with a sling. It was their only way of making a little money for a badly needed drink.

ALBERT

*

As long as I can remember, Albert lived in one of Barney's unused horse stables. Albert didn't mind the cobbled stone floor or lack of a fire. A bale of straw spread in the corner of the stable was good enough to keep Albert warm on a cold winter's night. He was a very quiet man and kept to himself. Nobody knew where he came from. It was the talk of the yard that he had been in jail twenty years for murder, but Dad said it was only a rumour, Albert wouldn't hurt a fly. One day he wandered into the bottle yard looking for work and since that day the bottle yard has been his home. Albert, an Aboriginal, had been with Barney ever since, as a caretaker and rouseabout. Albert didn't have many friends. He was a loner and people shied away from him. It didn't worry my Dad. There were days Albert came with us just to have a break from the bottle yard. There was no better stacker than Albert. He was the only one in the yard who could stack five dozen and two beer bottles in a sack bag. "Never worry about the colour of a man's skin. It's what's underneath that counts," said my Dad.

TWO BROTHERS

*

I liked these two brothers; one was married to my mother's sister. They were the best of mates and did odd jobs in the bottle yard. Except for the time I spent in the bottle yard, I had little contact with them. Sometimes I went to the hardware store in Victoria Street, just a few doors from the yard, to buy a bottle of methylated spirits for them, which they mixed with Coca-Cola. Cheap wine was not strong enough for them. I knew what I was doing. They weren't allowed in the shop to buy methylated spirits. After selling our bottles, we still had two more places to sell the rest of our goods. The New York Junk Yard in Gipps Street, Collingwood, was a very large building with a tin fence and was only a five-minute drive from the bottle yard. While Dad was selling the bath heaters and the brass we stripped from the iron bed, I sorted the woollies from the rags. It meant an extra threepence a pound we got for the wool at Plain's the rag buyers next door to the New York Junk Yard. While Dad sold the rags and woollies, I watched a worker in the big yard cutting up iron beds stacked sky high. Every time pieces of iron fell from the guillotine, a worker picked them up and filled a forty-four-gallon iron drum ready to be shipped to Japan. Our prime minister at the time, Sir Robert Menzies, was nicknamed Pig Iron Bob. Japan turned those bed ends into war machines against us. After what seemed a never-ending wait, my Dad appeared with a big grin on his face, holding the money in his hand. I jumped down from the cart as he added up the small change in his pocket. "Not bad Jumbo. We earned seven pounds for the morning's work. By the way, that was a good deal you did today. We got twenty-four shillings for the brass bed." That's what I loved about my Dad. He always made me feel important. Dad didn't have to tell me; it was always the same talk. "It's lunch time, Jumbo. You'd better take the horse and cart back to the bottle yard; I will be at the Town Hall pub." I liked nothing better than being in charge of the horse and cart, holding the reins as the horse trotted at a slow pace. For a shilling, I had plenty of thirsty helpers to bed the horse down for the night. I was in no hurry to go back to the pub; it was going to be a long day. Today Dad would have a lot of hangers-on looking for a free drink. It annoyed me the way Dad spent our hard-earned money. I decided to hang around the bottle yard and help to unload any cart that came in late. For a couple of hours' work I made two shillings for myself. Then on my way back to the Town Hall Hotel, I bought a pie and my favorite drink, a cold bottle of milk.

If I was Dad's guardian, he was rarely mine. Dad's two women played a very important part in my early life. There were times when Dad went to work, I was taken care of by one of these women. When I got older, I came to realise Dad had a trail of woman coming and going, just like the way we shifted house. Dad had a bad temper, more so when he was in his own home, especially with women who had lost touch with life. A cowardly punch, or maybe a black eye was a normal thing for them, as long as there was beer to drink, they suffered these indignities. I was not afraid when these scenes started. I thought they deserved to be hit. I wanted them to leave, then I would have Dad all to myself.

BAD THOUGHTS

*

We had just rented a house in Collingwood and Dad said, "We will stay here for a while." It was a Sunday morning, Dad and I were going to see Grandma when his mate Mocka, once a middleweight boxer who in his prime fought at Festival Hall, pulled up outside our house with a horse and cart. For a moment I thought we were going bottleoing even though it was a holiday. All thoughts of seeing Grandma were forgotten as we made our way to Richmond and stopped at the entrance of a dead-end lane. Dad got down from the cart and backed the horse and cart next to a factory door. I thought we were going to load the cart with scrap. I still wasn't too sure what was going to happen when Dad's mate climbed up onto the roof of the factory and Dad threw him a coil of rope. I was then bunked up onto the roof, Dad climbing up behind me. This was when I was told I was going to open the door. Dad ripped a sheet of tin off the roof. I looked down through the hole while the rope was tied around my waist. I wasn't a bit scared as I was lowered down onto the floor and threaded my way between stacks of cardboard boxes. All I had to do was climb up on a box and remove two crossbars, then open the top and bottom bolts. Dad and his mate loaded the cart with several boxes. It was all over in a matter of minutes, and then we made our way back to our house. I was old enough to know Dad and his mate had robbed a factory. Dad made me swear not to tell anyone, as we would all go to jail and the John Murray would be waiting for me.

A few days later, the cardboard boxes were taken away and that evening Dad came home with Mocka and a lot of money. Till that money ran out, there was no work, just drink, drink, and more drink. With his lady friends. Dad bought me a secondhand bike. It was my pride and joy. I had this urge to take out every street light. With my shanghai I rode my bike around the streets breaking light globes. I would look for a street light with a wire cage. A little hole no bigger than a twenty-cent coin was at the bottom of the iron cage. It was another challenge to me. I could still take out the globe by riding my bike under the street light without holding the handlebars, and ping the globe with a small ball bearing, then ride away to the next street as fast as I could.

SCROUNGING FOR FOOD

*

Although Dad often made a lot of money, he drank it away. I learnt at an early age how to survive hard times. When I woke up hungry and there was no food in the house, I often walked around the streets, looking for a bottle of milk left by the milkman. Just inside a front gate of a house. The baker's cart also provided me with a loaf of bread. I'd hide around the corner and wait for the baker to make his delivery. When it was the right moment, I'd make a dash for the cart door and grab my loaf of bread. The owner of the cake shop in Smith Street Fitzroy was a kind man. Once or twice a week, just on closing time, I'd go to the shop and ask for any vanilla scraps left on the cake tray. The shop keeper filled a brown paper bag for me. Then there were other days at lunchtime the Salvation Army in Wellington Street, Collingwood, served a bowl of hot soup and a bread roll.

FREE BREAKFAST

*

There is still a two-story brick building in Wellington Street, Collingwood. At the back of the building was a tin shed. Every Sunday morning, Dr. Singleton conducted a service and provided a free breakfast. Like a lot of other hungry people who came for the food and were in need of a jumper or a pair of shoes, I was one of them. Women and men, boys and girls, were already waiting for the tin shed doors to be opened when I arrived. Being a young and cheeky eight-year-old kid, I'd worm my way towards the shed door, as I wanted to sit in the front row to be noticed that I wasn't wearing any shoes. Around nine o'clock a man opened the double doors. There was a rush for the best seats. I was pushed through the doors by the force of the people and managed to get a front-row seat.

For the next few minutes, we all waited in silence. Then Dr. Singleton appeared from a side door and everyone stood up and started clapping. As Dr. Singleton walked towards the rows of wooden seats filled with hungry mouths, he faced his flock he then raised both hands. For the next half hour or so, Dr. Singleton conducted a service. First, we sang a hymn, Onward Christian Soldiers, and then we listened to a sermon about how lucky we were the Lord had provided us with his blessing this morning. There were thousands of starving people in this world who were not as fortunate as us. Then we said grace. Several ladies were now walking up and down the aisle, passing out plates of meat or jam sandwiches and hot tea served in tin mugs. For some people, it might be their first meal for a day or two. After we finished breakfast, we sang another hymn. The ladies had begun distributing parcels of clothing wrapped in newspaper. I watched with envy whenever a parcel was passed to a person sitting near me. Finally, a large parcel was placed in front of me. I ran my hand over the newspaper, feeling for the pair of shoes wrapped inside the clothing. Seventy-six years on, Dr. Singleton's two- story, grey stone building still exists in Wellington Street, Collingwood. The tin shed served its purpose long ago. Dr. Singleton not only provided a free breakfast for the poor, he also made his clinic available for the needy. His name is still scrolled across the fascia of his building.

Not far from Dr. Singleton's is a Catholic church. One Sunday morning, after having a free breakfast, I decided I would like to go to church and see what it was like inside. It was moments like this, when I saw a church, that reminded me of the time I burnt down the tree. For a while I stood outside the iron gates, holding my parcel, watching the well-dressed people being greeted by a priest. I plucked up enough courage to follow a man and a lady who seemed to know what they were doing. The priest stopped me and told me to wait a moment. When there were only the two of us, he took one look at me and said, "What do you want?" "I would like to go to church," I replied. I was told in no mean manner to go home. I was not allowed in the church because I was poorly dressed with no shoes. After that Sunday morning I said to myself, "Church is not for me."

MA MALONEY

*

At the top end of Brunswick Street, Fitzroy was Ma Maloney's café, where you could get a three-course meal for a very small amount of money. The yellow wooden tables with their wobbly stools, seated many a hungry mouth. The torn, check table cloths were partly covered with thick slices of bread, a bottle of tomato sauce, a half tin of plum jam, and two large salt and pepper shakers, all neatly arranged against the flaky calcimine wall. The brown worn lino hardly served its purpose anymore. Ma was a tough cookie but had a heart of gold if you did the right thing by her. Ma's trademark was a tea towel slung over her shoulder. She'd greet you with a toothless grin as she placed a huge bowl of steaming hot soup in front of you, followed by the roast of the day. If you walked away hungry, it was your own fault. Her roast dinners and steamed puddings had no equal.

Ma also owned a two-storey building just around the corner from her cafe. The bottom storey contained stables. With the help of her son, she rented out a horse and cart for five shillings a day. There were several flea-infested rooms above the stables, which she also rented out. Ma Maloney was a clever business woman. The down-and-outs who spent most of their time on the streets of Fitzroy depended on her for food and a bed for the night, and a horse and cart or a two- wheeled handcart, to collect bottles to survive a day longer. Ma's middle-aged son, Red, was a household name in Fitzroy before the Second World War. His reputation as a fearless street fighter was known far and wide. Red knew only one way to settle a dispute, with his fists. People have heard of Squizzy Taylor, the tough guy who roamed the streets of Carlton and Fitzroy, about the same time as Red. He was a coward compared to Red. Squizzy was a petty thief. He gained a reputation by shooting someone. The only thing Red did wrong was to drink too much beer.

FIGHT NIGHT

*

On Friday nights at the old Fitzroy Stadium, regular fights were held. If you were game enough to get into the ring and fight a three rounder, the reward was ten bob for your effort. Many a desperate father put up his hand to feed his family for the weekend. Dad was never frightened to put up his hand to earn ten bob. Red Maloney was the main attraction of the night and he took on all challengers. They came from surrounding suburbs just to say, "I fought Red Maloney." If Red finished a fight off quickly, he'd take on another challenger. It wasn't unusual for Red to have two or three fights in the one night. This was what the crowd had come to see, Red batter his opponent into the ground. If it wasn't for his drinking, Red Maloney could have been the best. Only a handful of living souls now remember what the name Red Maloney meant to Fitzroy back in those days.

MAKING MONEY TO SURVIVE

*

It was often up to me to get money for food, even though most days Dad made more money than we needed to live on. The average wage for an accountant was about four pounds, ten shilling a week. Dad could make that in two days, but his money was wasted on drink. With the life I was leading, I was good at making money. Nothing pleased me more than when I could give Dad some. My Dad was always teaching me how to make money. If it wasn't making a deal on the bottle cart, it was something else, like going down to the iron foundry with my billy cart to pick out the pieces of melted iron from the sand pits. After I filled two or three kerosene tins of iron, I'd make my way to the New York Junk Yard, and sell the metal for a shilling a kerosene tin. I also had another routine. At least once a week, I wandered into the city and sat in my usual spot, outside the Capitol Theatre in Swanston Street, dressed up as a swaggie. With an old blanket wrapped over my shoulders, a felt hat -covering half my face, a frying pan, and a blackened billy which I rattled, I really looked the part. People were either impressed with my appearance, or they felt sorry for me. I collected a fair amount of money and took it home to my Dad.

One day I was sitting outside the Theatre where an old man was playing his violin, his music case spread open on the footpath holding a few coins. He had a greying beard down to his waist and was standing close to the gutter as he played. I was doing very well; he was getting annoyed with me, as most of the coins were thrown my way. He soon told me to beat it. I wasn't looking for any trouble, so I decided to walk down to Young and Jackson Hotel and take my billy around to see if I could collect money from the drinkers in the bar. A rattle here and a rattle there, a lone coin soon attracted the drinkers and a generous hand would slip into a pocket. There were nights I was told to go home by a policeman.

NOT A BRASS ZOO

*

One Saturday morning, Dad was in the kitchen emptying out his pockets, "Not a brass zoo Jumbo. Get me the screwdriver, I'll have to bust the gas meter." Dad was good at busting the gas meter. He had a certain way of springing the lock, and all the pennies came tumbling onto the floor. We gathered the pennies and stacked them in shilling lots. "Never be greedy Jumbo. There will be a day when you will want to do it again." Dad took about half and put the rest of the pennies back in the tray. He slammed the tin tray back with a mighty bang. The gasman would never have known the gas meter had been rattled when he came to collect the pennies. There were times I saw the gasman walking along the street carrying a leather bag full of pennies. I guess the bag must have been heavy by the way he walked. The few shillings Dad managed to get from the gas meter was enough for a drink, or he might even be lucky and back a winner with the SP bookie, Sleazy, who operated a book in the lane next to the pub. Sleazy was too smart to be caught by the local police. On the corner of the lane a man called a nit kept watch. When he saw a police car coming, he stood on a wire attached to a bell at the other end, which rang where the bookmaker was taking bets. People who were having a bet disappeared into a backyard. The lane was deserted when the police car passed by. Dad seemed to be in a better mood now after busting the gas meter. It was about eleven o'clock when we left the house and made our way to the hotel. Dad's first drink was a glass of lemon squash to ease his hangover. For the next couple of hours I stayed with Dad until it was time for me to go to the football match and collect beer bottles.

EARNING MONEY

*

There were groups of supporters walking along the footpath, proudly displaying their football colours. Others were streaming across the road with little concern for the traffic, which was forced to a slow crawl. I had no trouble getting into the ground for nothing. I'd look for someone old enough to be my father and ask him to take me in on his member's ticket. Today Collingwood was playing my favorite team, Fitzroy, at home. I reckoned I'd have a good day collecting the empty beer bottles scattered around the ground. Maybe I'd make about ten bob which would please my Dad, and if Albert the Aborigine was in the bar playing his gum leaf, I might get an extra shilling or two for taking his hat around. Once inside the ground, I'd see Old Tom the bottleo and ask for a sack bag to collect the beer bottles, then work the outer part of the football ground where the heavy drinkers were. After I half-filled my sack bag, I'd sell the bottles to Old Tom, who paid sixpence a dozen. Old Tom said to me one day I collected more bottles than any of the other kids. By the end of the day, bags of bottles were stacked high just inside the front entrance of the football ground.

On the Monday, Tom would spend most of the day taking the bottles to the bottle yard. I once asked Dad, "Why don't you buy the bottles like Old Tom?" Dad laughed. "It's the only way he can make a mean quid. Old Tom has to pay the right price." Dad always had an answer, as if he was defending himself against someone who might be doing better. It was now time for me to go and see my friend Albert. Pushing my way through the crowded drinkers, in the distance I could hear him playing 'Swanee' on his gum leaf. Many times I'd tried but could never get the sound I was hearing now. Albert made a little hole in the center of the gum leaf, then placed the gum leaf on his tongue with his two fingers. He caught my eye. I knew what that meant. I picked up his old, worn hat from the floor, handed him the few coins from it, then started walking among the men in the bar, poking the hat in their direction. Men here and there threw in a coin. Others didn't look up from their drinks, as if I didn't exist.

My experienced eye made me walk to a group of men who'd had more than enough to drink. I started to flip the few coins in the hat, and this made them laugh. I didn't care, I just wanted their money. I wasn't disappointed. One of the drinkers threw several coins into the hat. I got more money from that group of men than the rest of the bar put together. I grabbed a few coins as I walked away and put them in my pocket. It didn't worry me one bit taking the money. I knew if Albert had the chance, he would do the same to me.

Taking the hat back, I placed it at Albert's feet. "How much did you pinch?" "Nothing," I answered. "You little bastard!" Those words didn't mean a thing to me. I knew Albert was more than satisfied with the money I'd collected. He bent down and gave me two bob with a grin. I knew the next time there was a football match, I would be doing it again. The few bob I'd pinched made my day. I now had twenty- two bob for my Dad. It was time for me to make my way to the pub. I decided to keep a few shillings for food just in case Dad didn't have any money. Back at the hotel, the first thing I saw was Dad sitting at the card table with a heap of money on it. I could see Dad had too much to drink. He didn't ask me how much I had earned. All he said was, "Here's a shilling Jumbo, buy yourself a sarp." Clutching my hard-earned money in my pocket, I made my way towards the bar thinking, "Tomorrow when Dad is sober, I will tell him how I took a few shillings from Albert."

A BED FOR THE NIGHT

*

When we were desperate for a bed, Dad sometimes went to Ma Maloney's stables for the night. There were several rooms above the horse stables. He soon found a drinking partner in one of the rooms. I was sitting on the bed listening to Dad's drinking mate talking about the fellow who'd died the night before, in the room next door to where I was to sleep. "During the middle of the night," he said, "I heard this gasping sound as if someone was choking. I didn't take any notice and dozed off to sleep. The next morning, we found this bloke hanging from the door handle. What we couldn't work out was how did all the blood stains get on the wall."

Naturally, I was petrified when Dad told me to go to bed. The story weighed heavily on my mind. Opening the door, I closed my eyes for a moment to avoid the blood stains. I didn't bother to get undressed. I tried to convince myself the bloke next door was only trying to frighten me, and there wasn't a ghost in the building. With these thoughts, I slipped further under the bedclothes. But the smell of the dirty blankets and the lack of fresh air forced me to come out from my hiding place, and as I took a deep breath, the lights of an approaching car lit up the room. In that instant, my eyes followed the light around the room, searching for the blood stains which didn't exist. Too late. I felt the warmth of a trickle run down my leg. Once again, I'd wet the bed. It's ok, I'd be sleeping in a different bed tomorrow night. Wetting the bed was nothing new to me, it was a part of my life. The worst time of sleeping in a wet bed is if we stayed too long in a one-bedroom apartment. There was nowhere to air the mattress. Maybe that's one of the reasons we moved from room to room. I remember the time we were renting a room in Fitzroy; Dad took the wet mattress out to the yard to dry. The bed wire was crawling with bugs between the two pieces of wood at the head and the foot of the bed. Quite often, I woke up during the night scratching my neck. In the morning there were red marks on me.

GORDON HOUSE

*

To me, it was just another one of Dad's wasted nights. Dad wanted to see a live show at the Tivoli Theatre, not something that happened very often. Dad was a little under the weather when we left the Rob Roy Hotel. For once, he had some money to buy a Chinese meal before we caught a cable tram into the city. We must have looked like a pair of vagabonds, sitting in the tram as it made its way down Bourke Street before stopping outside the Tivoli Theatre, Dad in his working overalls and me in my dirty clothes. The thought of looking dressed up never occurred to me. What was good enough for Dad was good enough for me. We managed to get tickets without much trouble and were made to sit in the very back row. Why my Dad wasted his time in coming, I don't know. In a matter of seconds, he was snoring his head off. I tried to keep him awake for fear of us being thrown out. More than once, an usher came flashing his torch in our direction. A boy about my age was the star attraction. He was playing the drums. Sitting next to my snoring dad, I kept thinking, "I wish it was me playing those drums." When we left the theatre, it was time for Dad to face the fact we had nowhere to sleep for the night. It wasn't too hard; Gordon House was in Little Bourke Street, just a couple of blocks away and we could rent a room for the night. Gordon House was a place for homeless men who could afford a shilling for a warm bed, rather than sleep in the park. It was around ten thirty when we arrived at there. The three storey, brick building was in darkness except for the room where the night watchman was sitting by an open fire. He asked me how old I was. Dad paid a shilling for the night and was handed the key to our room. "It's on the second-floor cobber and watch the stairs." At the bottom of the stairwell was a dim light hanging from a never-ending cord. We fumbled our way up the flight of stairs to the next landing, where another dim light was hanging. While Dad was looking for the number of our room, I couldn't resist the temptation of looking over the balcony rail. All I could see was a black hole. Then I looked up at the stars and felt they were within my reach. I searched the sky for The Pot. "It must be on the other side of the building," I thought. Dad was good at naming the different stars. Sometimes, when we were sitting around a campfire at night, Dad would look up at the stars and point his finger, "Jumbo, see those stars? They are called the Milky Way." Dad was cursing every match as it went out. His voice was getting louder. Soon he would be swearing. Then it went all quiet. I guess he found the room number. A faint streetlight shone through the bedroom window as I climbed into my bed, dreading the thought of wetting the mattress.

RATS BY THE DOZEN

*

The next morning, Dad rented a two - story house in Stanley Street Collingwood. It was in such bad condition the rent was only ten shillings a week. Dad said, "This will do us, we'll soon clean the rubbish up." The big backyard and the old stable were just what Dad needed for the horse and cart. It was about lunchtime when we started cleaning the piles of rubbish scattered around the lounge room. Rats were jumping out of the rubbish and we found a nest with little ones. The rats were so big, Dad said they must have been living here for years. We could also hear them in the wall cavities. Dad was concerned about the rats. He decided to go and see one of his drinking mates and borrow two ferrets to kill the rats. All afternoon we put the ferrets under the house and in the gaps between the walls. Judging by the noise and the squealing, the ferrets must have killed dozens of rats. I was to sleep on an old couch. "It will do until we pick up a bed the next time we go bottleoing," said Dad. The first night, Dad left the light on in the lounge room where I was to sleep, just in case there were more rats. He thought it was safer for me. I was terrified, listening to the rats scampering inside the walls. The noise was so loud I was too scared to go to sleep. I told Dad the next morning the rats frightened me and all he said was, "While the lights are on, they won't come out, and on the weekend, we will get rid of the rest." For several nights I listened to those rats before tiredness took over. Then it happened. Dad forgot about the rats and turned the light off while I was asleep. It must have been about midnight when I woke up screaming. I was trying to push the rats away from my face and arms. They were all over me and I was bitten several times before Dad heard me and came running out to the lounge room and turned the light on. The rats continued attacking me. They wouldn't leave my face and arms. I guess the blood must have sent them crazy. My Dad also got bitten on his hands as he tried to brush the rats away. I was in a real mess. Dad took me to Fairfield Hospital. I was there for about three weeks before I was allowed to leave. I remember walking across the hospital lawns with Dad as if it was yesterday when he said, "They forgot to give you your injection," and started to walk back to the hospital. I didn't want another one. I wanted to go home. Dad said, "the rat house was too dangerous to live in. We have moved to a room in North Melbourne." Usually we moved only a few streets away from the previous place because Dad liked to be close to the bottle yard and his mates.

I MISSED MY DAD

*

It was good to be back with my Dad. It didn't matter to me where I lived, as long as I was with him. Dad could never settle down and be like other men. He wanted to be someone and his drinking made him what he was. When Dad was on a bender, he sold whatever he had for more drink, even his horse and cart if he had one at the time. Nothing else mattered and soon we'd be looking for another place to live. I think he owed money to one of the publicans and had decided to lie low for a while. I liked the new place. It was on the second floor, with a balcony where Dad and I watched the passing traffic. Sometimes when a hansom cab passed by, I found myself envying the man sitting on the high seat as he loosely held the reins. I wished Dad owned a hansom cab like that. We could ride together. Maybe sometimes Dad might let me hold the reins. Then the sound of the horses clopping along slowly faded away, my fantasy fading with it.

Dad didn't bother about going over to Fitzroy to see his mates. He was content to go to Ma Kelly's bottle yard, just a couple of blocks from where we rented a room. Ma Kelly didn't hire out horses and carts like Barney did. In the bottle yard were several two-wheel carts lined up against the yard wall, waiting for anyone to take one for the day, free of charge, to collect bottles. It was hard work for Dad pushing the cart around the streets of North Melbourne. The cart had two long wooden shafts with a crosspiece attached to the front of the shafts. With a full load of bottles, it was a lot better for Dad to press his chest against the wooden crossbar and pull the cart with my help. Dad did these two or three times a day to sell his bottles.

ILL-TREATED

*

I was playing a game of cricket in the street and had started bullying one of the other kids if I didn't get what I wanted. I just took it for granted. It was the only way I knew how to survive in life. I didn't see Dad watching me from the balcony. Dad started to swear at me and told me to get inside. It was the first and only time Dad struck me in the face. I fell to the floor and received a push in the ribs. He was cursing me, telling me he would teach me not to bully those kids. For once, I wanted to get away from my Dad. I thought he was no better than anyone else and decided to run away before he woke up. Dad had more than enough to drink, so I waited for him to go to sleep, then grabbed a few clothes and put them in a hessian bag. Before I left, I went through Dad's pockets and took a little money for something to eat. I wasn't too sure what I was going to do; I just wanted to get away. My first thought was the cave. I could sleep there for the night and it was a safe place. I bought myself a bottle of milk and some fish and chips and ate them at the same time. I fiddled with the broken paper extracting a hot chip as I walked down Johnson Street to the Yarra River. I soon found myself threading my way through the bamboo sticks towards the cave. Satisfied with eating the last of the chips, I left my little bundle in the cave and wandered around the bottom of Dights Falls until it was getting dark. I never felt frightened or threatened in my cave. It was my secret hiding place. I climbed into my hessian bag and listened to the sound of a car and the clattering of horses' feet crossing the bridge. My thoughts drifted back to my Dad. "Why did he hit me?" I was only doing what he taught me.

Still determined not to go home, except for walking up to Johnson Street to buy something to eat for my breakfast, the Yarra River and its banks were my home for the rest of the day. Tired of playing, I decided I didn't want to sleep another night in the cave. As I wondered what I was going to do, I thought of the rooms above the stables and Albert at the bottle yard. The bundles of straw would keep me warm or I could walk over to Richmond and see my mother. Maybe she would take me in. The cave had more appeal. The next morning, I left the cave early and made my way back to North Melbourne and waited for Dad at the bottle yard. Not a word was said about what had happened two days ago, or where I had slept for the past two nights. Dad was just happy to see me.

MY OWN BOSS

*

As a young boy, I was my own boss. I did almost whatever I liked. Dad never bothered stopping me when I decided to go bush on my own. He had every confidence I could take care of myself; he bought me a second hand twenty-two short rifle, which I spent hours cleaning and polishing and pretending I was in the bush shooting rabbits. Dad showed me how to climb through a wire fence with a rifle always pointing towards the ground and with the safety catch on. I became a very good shot. We had just moved to a room in Park Street, Collingwood, only a few doors from the Bendigo Hotel. One Friday afternoon I decided to go bush for the night, shoot a few rabbits, and sell them to make some money. Dad gave me two shillings for my tram and train fare to Bacchus Marsh. Dad didn't believe in good bye kisses or hugs. I liked to travel as light as possible so only carried a hessian potato bag to sleep in, my rifle, a packet of fifty short bullets, a pocket knife to clean the rabbits, two slices of bread with butter if we had any and a box of matches. I was now ready to catch a cable tram to Spencer Street Station. I liked to sit up the front of the cable tram near the tram driver. Slowly, the tram came to a stop as he applied the brakes to a cable beneath the tram. Then he moved another lever and the tram slowly gathered speed. The driver repeated this whenever he wanted to start or stop the tram. The front carriage where the tram driver drove the tram was called the dummy and was the best part of the tram to ride in. If you didn't have any money for your fare, you could easily jump off the tram as it came to a stop. I caught the train at Spencer Street Station and arrived at Bacchus Marsh about an hour before sunset. This gave me enough time to follow the winding creek for about three miles and make camp for the night under a tree close by. It never occurred to me I might come to any harm, as I was never frightened of the dark. On my way, I shot a three-quarter grown rabbit for my tea. It was a perfect shot, right between the eyes. If I bruised the rabbit, I shot another one. It wasn't hard to find a good camping spot under a large tree close to the creek. It was just the right place to protect me from the wind, which was now blowing strongly. I was very experienced in the bush for a nine-year-old boy. Dad had taught me how to make a camp fire by scraping a hole in the ground and building a row of stones around the hole to protect the fire from the wind. While the fire was accumulating red coals, I skinned the rabbit and cut it into small pieces to cook for my tea.

As I sat around the campfire eating my rabbit, the chill of the night kindled my thoughts. I wondered, "Where is Dad now? If he is not at the pub when I get home in the morning, I will have to go to the police station and see if he is in the lock up." With my twenty-two-short rifle beside me, I soon fell asleep next to the fire. Several times during the night, I was woken by the noise of a water rat or a rabbit coming down to the creek for a drink. These noises never worried me. At the break of dawn, I woke feeling a little stiff, which was not a strange feeling for me. The few red coals that survived the night were soon ablaze with the support of a few dry twigs. It was enough for me to toast my piece of bread, which I partly burnt when the wooden twig I was using got burnt. Dad taught me so many things in life. I never forgot them.

Before I left the camp, I made sure the fire was out and the campsite was left clean. The early morning sun was telling me it was going to be a scorcher of a day and I had to be on my way. I guessed it was about six thirty. This gave me about three hours to shoot my quota of rabbits before I caught the train.

For the next four miles, I followed the winding creek, stalking rabbits at every bend. They would be idling in the morning sun, unaware of the shooter, unless I stood on a twig. The slightest sound made them dart into the clumps of fern, which gave them cover. If I had the advantage, I'd take careful aim for the head. If I missed and bruised the rabbit, I would leave it. By the time I got to the station, I had shot six pairs of rabbits. I was feeling pretty tired from the walk and carrying the heavy load and was glad to sit down and wait for the train, with the rabbits scattered at my feet. Soon the dead rabbits attracted dozens of small flies and I was kept busy brushing them away. People also kept their distance and gave me looks of disapproval. I was relieved to see the train appear. People still avoided me as I made my way towards an empty carriage and soon found a seat by a window. I guess seeing the rabbits sprawled over the floor kept people away. It was around ten thirty on Saturday morning when I arrived at Spencer Street Station, then caught the tram. I was hoping Dad would be waiting for me at the pub so I could show him my catch. There he was, sitting on the pub seat with his legs crossed, holding a five-ounce glass. I knew as soon as I saw the five-ounce glass; he was broke and waiting for me. At two shillings each for the twelve rabbits, they didn't last very long. Dad said to anyone who would listen, "'did you see all shot in the eye." That was enough for me. I knew I had pleased my dad. Once again, I sat beside him feeling the most important person in the bar, sipping away at my pot of sarsaparilla. All I wanted was to please; I didn't want to be rejected.

LOOKING AFTER DAD

*

You could say I was Dad's guardian. Whenever he had any money, I'd find him in the pub at the round table with no-hopers who would be looking for a free drink, pretending to listen to how Dad made four pounds for three hours' work. A down-and-out waiting for the right moment to catch Dad's eye with his empty glass in his hand trying to bot a drink. By the end of the day, all of my Dad's hard-earned money, or most of it, was spent on his so-called mates. Dad didn't exist in the minds of the hangers on, to them he was just an easy touch. As I got older, I became a lot wiser about my Dad. I learnt to keep some of the money. The routine was nearly always the same at closing time. My arm around Dad's waist to support him as we made our way home. Dad liked to sit at the kitchen table with his two bottles of beer. Then Dad would say, "Get me some fish and chips." While I was away, Dad usually fell asleep at the table. When he woke up, he'd be in no mood for fish and chips. In his drunken state he'd say, "Jumbo, get me the ferrets." We didn't always have ferrets. It only happened sometimes when Dad rented a house so we could go bush for a few days and catch rabbits.

In the darkness of the night I put my hand in the ferret cage, feeling for the back of their neck so I could grab their head. I was a little wary of the pole cat, as it had bitten me before. Dad liked to play with them on the kitchen table, putting them down his trouser legs and in his mouth. He once threw a ferret into the air, and it landed on his shoulder and gave him a nasty bite on the neck. Dad went into a rage and wrung its neck, then threw the ferret with all his force against the kitchen wall. Blood spattered everywhere. When he got tired of playing with the ferrets, once again he'd fall asleep at the kitchen table. It was my job to catch the ferrets and put them in their cage before I went to bed. The next morning, the first thing Dad did was to break two eggs into a beer glass partly full of vinegar smothered with pepper. This would fix his hangover, then he'd have breakfast before setting off to work.

BLACK MARIA

*

Every Saturday night, the police roamed the streets of Fitzroy in the Black Maria, looking for drunks. It was also their way of cleaning up the streets and trying to cut down on domestic violence. The large black van, with its over-sized wheels and little air vents along the top of the roof, looked like an armoured tank as it cruised around the streets. When the Black Maria suddenly appeared around the corner, if we were quick enough and near someone's front gate, we'd try to get onto the verandah before the police saw us. If they did, they would stop the Black Maria and come over and ask if we lived there. I would tell them yes. If they didn't believe me, the police knocked on the front door and checked. If you were lucky enough, sometimes people liked to help you. When people saw the Black Maria outside their door, they knew you were in trouble. There were times Dad didn't make it home. The police were not kind to drunks; they handled them roughly as they shoved them into the back of the van. Then they closed the large iron door with a terrific bang and locked it with a long sliding bolt. The people inside their houses knew some poor drunk was being locked up for the night. After Dad was taken away from me, I'd tried to follow the police van around the streets, seeing it stop every so often to pick up drunks who wanted to go home after a day in the pub. I am sure a newborn turtle had a better chance of surviving its run to the sea than those men had of dodging the Black Maria.

Whenever the van stopped and the door was opened, I'd try and see if I could get a glimpse of my Dad. If he was sitting at the end of the van, sometimes he gave me a wave. When the police van was full, it headed back to the police station and the men were charged for being drunk in a public place. Meanwhile, if I lost sight of the Black Maria, I'd go to the Fitzroy police station and wait for it to arrive. People would be standing next to the iron fence except for one or two like me who were concerned. Others were just onlookers, waiting for a side show to start, such as one of the drunks resisting the police. About twenty-five drunks were locked up for the night, those who couldn't raise the one-pound note for their bail stayed locked up for the weekend. My Dad would sing out, "Get me bail Jumbo." If he didn't have any money, I tried to get it myself. Otherwise, he faced court on the Monday, which meant spending another two days in the clink.

More than once, if I was a few bob short, I'd put on my swaggie's gear and rattle my billy outside the Regent Theatre in Johnson Street, Fitzroy. If I couldn't get the money, Dad was locked up till the Monday morning. The judge sometimes handed down a fine or a small sentence. My Dad more than once spent a few days as a guest of His Majesty because of his drinking.

THAT MAN AGAIN

Working on the bottle cart came to a temporary end when Dad had another visit from the man in the grey suit. This time he handed Dad a piece of paper. It was Dad's last warning. I had to go to school. This time Dad decided he would take me to school himself. I went to Victoria Park State School for the next few weeks. Between wagging and the occasional days with Dad on the cart, I managed to keep the man in the dark suit away. School to me, was a waste of time; I only wanted to be on the bottle cart with my Dad.

GOING BUSH WITH DAD

*

I liked going to the bush by myself but loved it when I went with Dad. He'd dry out for a few days and we'd have a lot of fun together. Of course, it was yet another reason why my schooling kept getting interrupted. One day, Dad started talking about spending a week in the bush. He said if he put some money together, we'd go for a week. I felt jumpy as I stood beside the bar. I was too nervous to hold my pot of sarsaparilla. I had to rest it on the bar counter while we waited for the race to start. One of the drinkers shouted for the publican to turn the wireless up; the horses were just about to jump. The thought of listening to the race turned my stomach into knots. Dad cursed his mate for talking as we tried to listen to the race above the noise in the bar. I couldn't catch the name of the horse. I was watching my Dad's face. Finally, it told me what I wanted to know. I saw Dad hit the table hard with his fist and look over at me. "We won Jumbo. Go to the stable and get the horse and cart. We're off to the bush son." I ran most of the way to the stables. The thought of being in the bush for a week with Dad excited me. It wouldn't take me long to put the harness on Dolly. It was something I did most mornings. "Dad and I are going bush!" I thought, as I drove the horse and cart back to the house. I knew I had lots to do before I came back to the pub. First the ferrets would have to be fed, then l gathered up blankets, kitchen things, a few clothes and whatever I thought we needed. I decided not to wait at home for Dad, instead take the horse and cart to the pub. Dad was leaning against the pub wall talking to his mate, Mocka. By the look of them, they were both very much under the weather. I managed to push my way through the crowd of drinkers who were packed six deep around the bar. To get Dad's attention, I gave a sharp tug on the sleeve of his coat, "Come on Dad, the horse and cart's outside." But it didn't matter. Whatever I tried; he would not budge until the hotel doors closed. At last, Dad and his mate staggered out of the pub with an armful of bottles. Dad said, "Jumbo, take me to Wildwood." With my help, they somehow managed to pull themselves up on the cart. Soon they were snoring their heads off. It was still light when I stopped outside a shop in Alexander Parade, Essendon and searched Dad's pockets for money to buy a few things we needed for the trip; food, tobacco and matches for Dad. As I drove away from the shop, I realised it was about another six or so miles to the Essendon Airport and then there would be little traffic on the road to Wildwood. I remember on one of our trips to Wildwood as we passed the Essendon Airport, we saw a plane which had crash- landed on the side of the road. Dad said it was a D C 3. At the time, it meant very little to me.

I loved driving the horse and cart on a trip like this. I felt safe with my Dad asleep next to me. It gave me a comfortable feeling. Our horse would trot along at a steady gait and there was no need to push her. It was a fairly long trip, about a two-hour drive from Fitzroy. Dad had taught me to let the horse bowl along at its own pace. I just gave him his head and reminded him occasionally with a flap on the rump, to keep his mind on the job. I was lucky it was such a beautiful night for travelling. The stars were out in full, the stillness of the night only broken by the sound of Dolly clopping along. At last we reached the sign which said Wildwood. A few miles further on was a small township called Sunbury where we had camped many a times, doing what we liked best. In time, Sunbury was to be the turning point in my life, and for the better. A few hundred yards from the Wildwood Bridge was a steep incline. I was a little scared at the thought of taking the horse and cart down the steep incline by myself. I decided to stop and wake my Dad up to do it. But no matter how hard I shoved him and Mocka, I couldn't wake them. They were still too drunk from their day's drinking. I either had to park on the side of the road until Dad woke up or take the horse and cart down myself. I knew what to do; I had watched and helped Dad many times before. First, I locked the back wheel with the chain we used to lock the back wheels whenever we left the cart unattended. Then, I held Dolly firmly with the reins as we descended the steep cutting. Dolly's back legs were holding hard against the breaching strap, which was there to prevent the cart pushing the horse down the hill. With one wheel locked and Dolly's strength, we finally made the descent. I rested the horse for a few minutes. When I look back now, I wonder how many boys my age would have known what to do.

In the still of the night I was feeling very sleepy so I decided to make camp under the bridge. The frogs croaking in the creek bed, a rustle in the bushes close to where I stopped, was either a fox hunting his nightly meal, or a rabbit I might have disturbed. These noises in the night never worried me as I had my Dad to protect me. I unfastened the lamp from under the cart to give me a little light in the darkness and made my way to the creek to fill the bucket with water. That's when I saw the yellow eyes of a fox. This made me stand still and watch him for a moment. The fox looked towards the light; I think it must have picked up my scent because he retreated to safety. If only I had my rifle. I then unharnessed Dolly, tied her to the back of the cart with one of the reins and gave her a well-earned drink before bedding her down. I was more than ready to slip under the blanket and cuddle into my Dad; it was a nice feeling. Dad's voice woke me, telling Mocka to get some more firewood. The first thing I saw when I opened my eyes were the rays of the sun peeping through the cracks of the red gum sleepers, which had worn away over the years. Just for a moment, I looked out from under the blanket and my mind was filled with excitement for what lay ahead of me. We were right next to the creek, with fresh water flowing past our camp and plenty of firewood lying close by. The smell of breakfast cooking on the open campfire sharpened my appetite for a hearty breakfast. Just a short walk from the blue stone bridge, was a farm where two sisters, Maggie and Ethel, lived. The farm house was badly in need of repair and a good paint. The front verandah had sunken beyond repair and now was hanging by its last threads. It seemed to be a part of the sisters who did their daily chores in their long aprons and high boots. Their best years had been lost looking after their aged parents, who had now passed away. Whatever pleasure they got out of life now, my father was a part of it.

They were a landmark in the district. Every morning and in the evening as the sun was starting to set, you would see Maggie or Ethel walking along the road with their dog, a twisted stick directing their small herd of cattle towards the milking shed. Neither sister had married. Dad had become more than friendly with them when we first started camping by the creek. He'd gone over to their farm one morning to ask for some milk. It took me a while to realise it was a waste of time to go looking for him. We had finished our breakfast and Dad said he was going over to Maggie's to get a billy of milk. "I won't be long," he said as he walked off, gleefully swinging the billy to and fro. He looked back, "Keep the fire going. We'll have a cupper." Mocka gave me a big grin. He wasn't interested in going with Dad. All he wanted was to open a bottle of beer. Mocka was not like my Dad. When Dad decided to go bush, drinking was the last thing on his mind. It was his way of drying out for a few days and being the Dad I wanted. Maggie and her sister saw the best side of Dad. Mocka and I decided to fill the morning in by taking the ferrets and catching a few rabbits. It wasn't long before we found a rabbit burrow with a trail of fresh droppings. The ferrets were keen to work. Soon we heard rabbits running for cover or being trapped in the nets and it wasn't long before we had more than enough rabbits.

It was now close to midday and the sun was beating down on us. Mocka suggested it was time we made our way back to camp as soon as the ferret came out of the burrow. We waited for another half an hour and still there was no sign of the ferret. "It must have gone to sleep, or a rabbit has blocked it in," Mocka said. "Let's light a fire at the entrance of the burrow to see if the smoke will make it come out." Eventually the ferret poked its head out of a pop hole we had missed putting a net on. I grabbed a dead rabbit and teased the ferret away from the hole until it was safe to grab it behind the neck. Its mouth was covered in blood and fur. The size of the ferret's stomach told you it had a good meal and was contented to sleep it off.

NO SIGN OF DAD

*

It was well after lunch time when we arrived back at the camp. Dad was nowhere to be seen. Mocka remarked with a big grin on his face, "I guess Bob had to wait till the cows came home." Before we had our lunch, we gave the ferrets a drink and gutted the rabbits. To protect the rabbits from the flies, we hung them on a branch and covered them with a chaff bag. The bottles of beer had been in the creek for several hours now and Mocka was dying for a drink. After drinking two bottles of beer, Mocka soon fell asleep.

With my shanghai I spent the rest of the day stalking rabbits and birds. It was not until late in the evening, when I was sitting around the camp fire with Mocka and feeling very sleepy, Dad appeared out of the dark carrying the billy of milk. My sleepiness suddenly disappeared. I wanted to hear what Dad had to say. Not a word was said about being away all day. Mocka made Dad a piece of toast and I lifted the billy off the fire and topped it up with more water to brew him a cup of tea. While I was doing this, I heard them laugh. I guess Dad must have been talking about his day with Maggie. It was all quiet, and I felt the chill of the air against my back competing against the warmth of the fire for a part of me, when Dad pointed to a cluster of stars. "See that one Jumbo? That's the Milky Way, and the one above your head is the Pot," and he kept talking about the stars. I had heard all this talk before. I was tired and wandered off to bed.

The next morning, I was awakened early by the crackling of the fire and Mocka's voice. Once again, the fragrance of burnt toast drifted toward me as I lay between the blankets. I was hungry, and I soon joined Dad and Mocka around the camp fire for a hearty breakfast. Later, I helped Mocka to carry the dirty dishes to the creek and wash them, while Dad gave the ferrets a drink of milk.

"Never give them a proper meal before you work them, Jumbo," Dad said. "They'll go to sleep on a full stomach." It was my job to count the rabbit nets and put them back in the carrying bag while Mocka cleared the camp and Dad put out the fire. These were some of the happiest memories of my childhood, walking over the hills with my Dad, knowing he wouldn't be drunk today. As we left the camp Dad said, "Let's try a couple of burrows at the second gully. The first gully is too close to the road." There was not a sound of a rabbit being chased by the ferrets. It was then Dad said Maggie had told him to work the third gully. Now I realised why we had walked so far. It took us another ten minutes to reach the third gully. Before we found a burrow with fresh rabbit droppings, straight away we heard a rumble. I was very quick at catching a rabbit when it got caught in a net. I wanted to please Dad and show off in front of Mocka. More than satisfied with our catch, Dad said, "It's getting too hot for the ferrets. Let's pack up." As we left the last gully behind us, no one was more pleased than me to see the bridge in the distance. I seemed to get a new lease of life. Forgetting all about the weight of the rabbits, I raced towards the camp for a much-needed drink of cold running water.

Even though it was only midday, our day was far from finished; we still had work to do before we could relax and have something to eat. Dad and Mocka started to skin the rabbits and stretch the skins on wire we managed to scrounge from a broken fence near the creek. My job was to clean out the ferret boxes and change the bedding with dry grass, then feed the ferrets their bread and milk. Later, Dad gave them a couple of the rabbit livers, and I lit the fire, and while the billy boiled for our tea, we had a dip in the creek. I knew Dad was freshening up before he made his way over to Maggie's, but it was fun splashing in the water with him.

I loved playing with my Dad. I wasn't happy with him when he said he was going to the store with Maggie to get supplies and I was to stay and help Mocka make wire cages for the live rabbits we were going to catch the next day. I wanted to go with him. To make it worse, as soon as Dad left with the buggy, Mocka made for the creek and pulled out two bottles of beer, then sat under the shade of the tree, contentedly drinking before dozing off into a deep sleep. It was late again when Dad arrived back from Maggie's. I wasn't happy with him for being left alone for most of the day. I knew Dad must have sensed it when he said, "Jumbo, tomorrow we'll have a big catch, and in the afternoon, we'll go over to Maggie's and you can help her with the milking." I was happy now, and didn't mind when Dad said, "Fill the billy. We'll have a cup of tea." After a while, I went to bed, leaving Dad and Mocka to talk about his day with Maggie. Dad was never wrong when he said we will have a big catch. Several times Mocka had to walk back to the camp with the rabbits. Dad was more than pleased with the morning's catch. After a meal and a rest, it was time to go and help Maggie and Ethel with the milking. The cows were already waiting in the yard, and while I helped Maggie, Dad and Mocka headed for the wood heap and chopped up enough wood to last Maggie for several weeks. We had just about finished milking the last two cows when Maggie said to me, "How would you like to stay and have some tea with us?" I was excited at the thought of staying and ran yelling to the wood heap to tell Dad. For some reason, Dad went inside with Maggie's sister Ethel and helped her with the tea. If only he could be like this all the time, helping women instead of belting them.

TABLE MANNERS

*

At the dinner table, I sat next to Ethel. I was very shy as I tried to eat my dinner with my knife and fork. I found it a lot easier to shovel the food into my mouth. Dad had never taken any notice of the way I ate, or shown me how to do it, but Ethel must have been watching me struggle. In her kind way, she showed me how to place my finger on the back of the fork and how to hold the knife. It was all too much for me. I soon went back to my old way of eating, feeling hot and flustered with each mouthful and finding it hard to swallow as Ethel watched me. I just wanted to leave the table and run back to the camp. We didn't have to worry about a white tablecloth or a knife and fork. Just before it started to get dark, Dad asked Maggie if he could have some of the wire netting he saw near the stables to make some wire cages to keep the rabbits alive. I could see Dad was anxious for us to leave. Mocka took the hint. "Come on Jumbo, we had better feed the ferrets before it's too dark." The rest of the week went quickly. After five days of catching rabbits, all of the wire cages were full. On the last day, Dad decided to take it easy as the ferrets were tired and we needed to be fresh for the trip back to Melbourne. I hated to hear those words but found plenty to do while Mocka finished off the last of the beer and Dad spent the last few hours at Maggie's farm. The next morning, we were all up early. I had a good breakfast of fried eggs and toast before we packed up and cleaned the camp site. The rabbits were left until last to kill. Dad pressed his penknife under the chin of a rabbit. Moments later, it was dead. Mocka was waiting to take out the innards of the rabbit. My job was to make a small cut in one of the rabbit's back legs, then pair them together. Dad said by doing this, it was the best way to keep the rabbits fresh. We had now been away eight days and although Dad had been with Maggie most of the time, it was one of the best weeks I'd had with my Dad in the bush. As we drove back over the bluestone bridge, Maggie and her sister Ethel were standing on the lean-to verandah. I felt sad as we passed. I thought if Dad lived there with Maggie, he wouldn't need a drink. I liked Maggie. She was not like the other women in Dad's life, except Violet. But I knew it was a passing dream. As Dad drove the horse up the steep cutting, Mocka and I walked behind the cart to lighten the load and as we rounded the bend, I took one last look. The sisters slowly disappeared. It was the last I ever saw of them.

It was around lunch time when we pulled up outside the Rainbow Hotel, which was on the corner of Gipps Street and Rockery Street, Collingwood. With our cart parked outside the hotel, it was not long before all the rabbits were sold. I was thinking to myself as I took the horse back to the stable, "Dad's going to have his first drink in more than a week. It's going to be a long afternoon."

AGAINST THE ODDS

*

Since our wonderful week in the bush, Dad, for the past two weeks, had been drinking a lot more than usual. Not going to work most days and spending his time with a woman he had picked up at the Rob Roy Hotel. He even sold the horse and cart and we moved to a small flat in Napier Street, Fitzroy. We were on our way home from the Rob Roy Hotel when the Black Maria appeared suddenly out of nowhere. We were lucky. We managed to turn into a laneway and saw it pass by, but if I had known what lay ahead of us, I would have been more than happy to see Dad picked up to spend the weekend in the clink. He was in a mean mood. All the way home, he was cursing. This woman was nothing more than a moll. We weren't far from home when he decided to cut through a vacant block. As we picked our way through heaps of rubble, he continued to curse his new woman. A few moments later, we arrived at a small, single-fronted house with a wooden picket fence. The door was slightly ajar. Without knocking, he walked down the passage way. I followed behind, not knowing what to expect.

There, sitting at the table drinking beer, was his woman with two Aboriginal men. Dad started to abuse them about having it off with his woman. A fight broke out and Dad got the worst of it, though both men were more concerned with getting Dad out of the house than fighting him. On the way home, Dad said, "Jumbo, we'll fix the bastards up!" A few hours later, Dad sobered up a little but was still brooding over his woman. I was told to get the axe from the shed. Off he went again, swearing and cursing the bastards as he carried the axe over his shoulder. I followed behind. I had to be with him because I didn't want him to get hurt. When we arrived at the house, the front door was open; I felt it was beckoning us to come in. Dad stood at the front door, yelling to the bastards to come out and fight him. He then went and stood in the centre of the road with the axe held in both hands.

The two Aboriginal men came out. Each tore a wooden paling off the front fence, large rusty nails jutting out from the ends. They began to circle Dad, each waiting for a chance to strike. My Dad threw a couple of blows with the axe. He missed. Immediately, the two of them rained blows on him. I picked up a piece of wood and tried to hit one of them but received a smack on the legs for my efforts. This sent Dad into a rage. Swinging wildly with the axe, he cut one man badly on the arm. The man dropped his fence paling and ran inside the house, holding his arm. Dad was now on the ground, with me screaming at the other man to stop. He must have taken notice of me and went inside the house.

SAINT VINCENT HOSPITAL

*

I helped Dad to his feet. I could see he was badly hurt. I looked over to the house and saw his woman standing at the door with the man who was not hurt. They were shouting and cursing us as we walked away. Dad was bleeding from several nail cuts; but he was a tough old bastard, more concerned with yelling back than his bleeding, which wouldn't stop. I took him to St. Vincent's Hospital, just a couple of blocks from where we lived. The bleeding seemed to get worse as we walked to the hospital. Dad was badly cut and was kept in hospital for most of the night. I was told to go home, but refused, saying I wanted to stay and wait for my Dad. When the nurses realised I wouldn't budge, I was given a rug, sandwiches and a hot drink, and assured my Dad would be all right. I soon fell asleep. Sometime later, I was awakened by a nurse. I didn't know where I was for a moment, then remembered the fight. Dad was standing next to the nurse, most of his face and arms covered in bandages. Then the doctor appeared, saying, "You should stay longer, you've lost a lot of blood." But Dad would have none of it. He wanted to go home. The nurses were really kind to me. As we were leaving, one of them held my hand. We arrived home to discover, much to my joy, Dad's woman had been to the house and taken all her clothes. Two days later, after selling his load of bottles, Dad was at his drinking hole telling his mates how he got one of them with the axe.

VIOLET

*

Violet always appeared with her case of clothes whenever Dad decided to go on the square, which was not very often. Sometimes Dad sent me to school while it lasted. You'd think Dad was starting a new life and the past was well behind him. I looked forward to coming home from school, my Dad in the backyard doing an odd job. I liked Violet; she was a caring person. She had her moments with drink, but when she and Dad were together may be for several weeks or longer, it was the only time I felt I was wanted. Most nights we had a hot meal for our tea, maybe a roast and a bread-and-butter pudding. It was something different from a Chinese meal or going to bed on an empty stomach. For once, I had clean clothes. Violet went to no end of trouble to make the place look nice. She always set the table with a cloth and we all sat down together to have our tea. Even my mattress was taken out to the backyard to dry. I could look forward to a dry bed, a feeling I very seldom experienced. In the past, there were times when my bed got so wet the urine rotted the wire and the bed mattress would hang through the gaping hole. At night I would dread going to bed; I was like a dog cast out into the night trying to find a dry spot to lie on. There were also times when the bed was crawling with brown bugs between the two pieces of wood at the head of the bed. The next morning, red spots covered parts of my body and legs.

After our tea, we all sat around the kitchen table and listened to our serial on the radio. My father loved to listen to Dad and Dave and he was always cursing Bill, Mabel's father. "If I could get my hands on that bastard, he wouldn't talk to me like that." Being a kid, I thought everything you heard on the wireless was real. When the serial finished, Dad would say, "Let's have a game of crib, Jumbo." Dad taught me how to play cribbage, a card game which uses a brass plate attached to a wooden board, for scoring. There were one hundred and twenty holes inserted in the brass plate for keeping a record for points you won. The first to one hundred and twenty won the card game. I went to bed feeling contented with my day, hoping tomorrow would be the same. The crib board was the only thing Dad treasured. Whenever I polish the crib board now where it is placed on our hall stand, it reminds me of my Dad and the happy times we spent playing crib together. Dad stayed off the drink for several weeks until one day I came home from school and found he and Violet were not home. I went looking for my Dad. It wasn't too hard. They were at the Napier Hotel. That night there was a big row. Violet received a black eye. The next morning, Violet packed her few things and left. It was not long before we were back to our normal life.

SUNDAY MORNING

Sunday mornings it didn't matter to me if it was rainy or sunny. I loved Sundays because it was the day my Dad was a real Dad. He never drank on a Sunday. He'd cook my breakfast, that's if he had any money left from his drinking. If not, he would send me down to the milk bar to pick up food, smokes, and a bag of boiled lollies. For breakfast, Dad cooked bacon and eggs with two thick slices of toast oozing with butter. This would bring a smile to our faces. When we'd finished breakfast and washed the dishes, we would go out to the backyard and do our odd jobs. I loved these moments with Dad. He'd sit down on his wooden box; I'd sit on the ground next to him and we talked about the things we had done together. He loved to reminisce. "Remember the time Jumbo, we lived in Marine Parade?" I remembered it very well. Across the road from where we lived were the police barracks and there was something like forty or so cadets in training. I became very friendly with the cadets and sometimes played football with them in the big yard next to the Drill Hall. Then one day Dad got into a fight at the local pub and got locked up for the night. The next day he got drunk again and all the way home he cursed the cadets. He was going to fix up those bastards. He said, "They gave me a couple of whacks while I was in jail." When we got home, he went straight to the bedroom and got the rifle from the top of the wardrobe. I clung onto his arm crying, "Don't, Dad." I was frightened for him. I ran over to the barracks. The cadets came over to the house and calmed Dad down and put him to bed. They took my rifle away for a few days, then gave it back to Dad because it didn't have the bolt action in it. That was my Dad, always getting himself into trouble when he got drunk.

GRANDMA

*

Grandma lived most of her life in a two-storey brick house in Fitzroy. I always remember the long narrow hallway that led to the tiny kitchen, with a small window which faced a shoe factory, across a rear laneway at the end of her small backyard. On hot days, or when workers were loading or unloading a truck, two large wooden doors were opened. From the kitchen window, you could see dozens of workers standing at their machines working away, quite oblivious to someone watching them from Grandma's kitchen window. Grandma was a self-taught artist. Both sides of the hallway walls were covered with her paintings. Two paintings of hunting dogs in large wooden frames were my favourites. Sunday was the only time Dad was allowed in Grandma's house. We never stayed very long because the rest of the family thought he shouldn't be allowed there. Dad was the black sheep of the family. Grandma was the only one that talked to Dad. It was her house and her son. He'd been a big disappointment to her in the way his life had turned out, yet she still loved him as a son. Sometimes as we sat in Grandma's tiny kitchen, waiting for the cast-iron kettle on the wood stove to come to a boil for Dad to have a cup of tea, we could hear Dad's brother talking to the others about us from the lounge room. My older brother and sister wouldn't come out but hid like the rest of them. I had no feelings for any of them. Listening to their voices, I just hated them, a feeling which lasted for most of my life. Dad knew if he went into the lounge room and caused trouble, Grandma would tell him to get out of the house and not come back.

SUNDAY WITH GRANDMA

*

But most times when we visited Grandma on a Sunday, everyone was away camping or fishing. That's when I liked being at Grandma's the best. We always came away with home-made cakes and goodies. On our way home, Dad would point out different buildings to me and explain what they were used for. "You see that two-storey building with the pulley hanging above the little door?" I looked up and knew what he was going to tell me. More than once I had stood beside the team of draught horses watching two men at work. One of the horses was unyoked from the wagon and a long rope attached to a special harness. A worker tied the other end of the rope around a bag of flour and give a command to the horse. It would walk several paces, then stop of its own accord. The bag of flour wobbled in the air towards the worker standing next to the open door. With one outstretched hand, he'd grab the rope and pull the bag of flour onto the second-floor platform. Then waving his hand, the man on the wagon sang out, "Back Betty," and the rope slowly descended down to the waiting man. This was repeated many times until the whole wagon was unloaded.

LEARNING THE TRADE

*

As usual, Dad and I were sitting at the table with Mocka, Darcy and Bullant, his drinking mates. They all earned their living bottleoing around Fitzroy or Collingwood, picking up anything of value. After selling their wares, the local pub was their next stop for a good yarn about their day's dealings and a good four-handed game of cards. Dad had a fist full of money from his morning's work. I was sitting next to my Dad, watching the cards, when Mocka piped up, "I made a quid today." Mocka only drank the cheapest of wine. When he asked the barman for a wine Mocka would say, "I'll have a four-penny dark mate." On the bar counter, a one-gallon wooden keg of cheap wine served its purpose. A clown could have worn Mocka's battered, purple, spongey nose with pride. In all, not a pretty sight, but that was Mocka. I was all ears as Mocka started to tell about his deal. "Pound my arse," roared Darcy. "You couldn't make a quid as long as you have a hole in your arse."

They were all a little frightened of Darcy, as he'd sooner have a fight than a feed. "Fair go, Darcy, I did make a quid. I got four bags of bottles and a bag of rags. I only paid her six bob for the lot." "Too much," said Darcy. "Two bob was more than enough for a deal like that." There was a little chuckle. We all knew Mocka was not a good dealer. Meanwhile, Dad was getting impatient, he wasn't a good listener. "For Christ sake Mocka, deal the cards. Bullant, it's your shout. Get my boy a sarp," his word for sarsaparilla. Gee, I was proud of my Dad, the way he bossed them around.

Then Darcy started to tell about his deal. "I had a good day. I was working near Yarra Falls Woollen Mill when I ran into old

Mack. You know him, always looking for a sling. He had slipped away from work for a quick nip. That bastard can't go for more than an hour without wetting his lips. It was a lucky break for me. He said there was a load of steel down at the back of Yarra Falls. He wasn't wrong. I picked up a ton and a bit of brass. You should have seen the way old Charlie dug in and pulled that load." My Dad ignored this remark. He was a little jealous of Darcy's horse. He looked at Bullant. "Where did you work today, or did you get tied up with Dirty Flo?" Flo's man was a bottleo like the rest of his mates. Light Fingers, as he was known to his mates, couldn't resist the temptation of a stack of bottles if the lady of the house wasn't home. He spent more time as a guest of His Majesty than sleeping in his own bed. Not that it was ever cold when he was away. There was always a bottleo's horse tied to Flo's paling fence. Bullant, who was knee high to a grasshopper, snapped back, "Fair go, Bob. You can get a woman anytime. I have to take what's offering. It's just that I was working close by and I found the going a bit slow." "Bet you didn't find Dirty Flo too slow," remarked Darcy. "My nag kept heading towards her joint," said Bullant. Darcy looked up from his cards and muttered, "It's had enough practice to know its way blindfolded, like any other nag in Collingwood."

Bullant pretended not to hear the remark. For a few moments, it was all quiet. Dad had been waiting for this moment. He knew he was the best. It was magic to listen to my Dad and watch the others grasp on to every word. Slowly, he began, "My hangover tonic wasn't working too well. I was going to stay home. Jumbo didn't want to go to school. He had already yoked up the horse and cart. I decided to have an easy day and work close to the bottle yard. In the first hour, we only pulled a few bags of bottles. I was just about to give the game away for the day when a little girl appeared, 'Mister, mummy has some bottles for you!' Well you could have knocked me down with a feather. Staring me in the eyes were these batteries, worth at least ten quid. I knew someone had been collecting them by the way they were stacked. I decided not to make my move just yet."

The other bottleos now couldn't take their eyes off my Dad. They knew when it took him this long to talk about a deal, it would be a good one. "I was filling the bag with bottles," Dad went on, "when the old girl started to tell me her life story about having to move into this house and was left with a dirty yard to clean up.

'They promised to come back,' she told me, 'I know it will be the last I will ever see of them. I am fed up with this mess. Those rotten batteries are stopping me from starting my vegetable garden.'" My Dad leaned back on his seat. "Now Mocka, I have been trying to teach you for years how to pull a good deal. The only time you earn a quid is when you jockey for me." My Dad knew Mocka would never understand, and it was his way of making him feel as if he was one of them. Dad gave me a wink and I knew I was going to be a part of the deal. He stopped talking for a moment and picked up his pot of beer. He wasn't in any hurry. The best was to come. He took another mouthful of beer and wiped his mouth with the back of his hand. "I knew the batteries were already mine."

You could have heard a pin drop, so intent were the others. King Bob took another mouthful. But Mocka had had enough, "For Christ's sake, Bob, what happened?" My Dad said, "So I said to her, 'Look lady, I don't usually do this, I only collect bottles. But seeing you are stuck with a dirty yard, I will clean it up for a quid. There are at least two loads to the tip. With the quid tucked away in my pocket and a load of batteries, I raised my hat and bid the lady farewell. Now Mocka, this is where I put the icing on the cake. I sent Jumbo back to get five bob for the tip fees. I could hear her putting on an act, but my boy didn't let me down. That kid is a born bottleo." I felt thirty foot tall. I couldn't down my pot of sarsaparilla quick enough. "Did you see the way he swigged that pot down?" my Dad said, "He's going to be a real boozer." He threw a note on the bar counter. "The drinks are on me boys." Gee, I was proud of my Dad, he loved these moments talking about his deals, being the centre of attention, and the bottleos praising him. He was the king of all the bottleos. They knew they wouldn't have to buy a beer for the rest of the day, as long as my Dad had money to throw around.

I REMEMBER THAT DAY

*

A good bottleo took pride in looking after his horse. If the horse shied at a piece of paper blowing across the road, it would soon find its way to the knackery for pet food. My Dad taught me a bottleo' s horse had to be strong, have a good temperament and above all, know how to respond to a command. My Dad had his eye on a certain horse. "Jumbo, when I win some money, I will pay Barney ten pounds for that horse." Dad did win money playing cards and bought the horse. We called our horse Darkie. Its shining black coat and powerful chest looked out of place, pulling a bottleo's cart. It wasn't that Bullant and Buck didn't have good horses, but Darkie was strong and was a natural pulling a cart. He was special and caused a lot of jealousy. My Dad was always talking about how good Darkie was. There wasn't another horse in Collingwood like Darkie. Buck was fed up listening every day to King Bob. He waited for a moment and said, "This morning I decided to work the back lanes of Carlton and before long I had one of the best loads I'd had for weeks. I was heading back to the bottle yard with a big load when Twinkle decided she wouldn't have a bar of it. In a flash, she took off and made for home. Twinkle was going so fast I couldn`t slow her down, even with the brakes full on. You should have seen the smoke; the brakes were so hot they nearly caught on fire."

I was watching my Dad. He didn't like what he was hearing. To try and stop Buck from holding the floor, he threw a ten-shilling note on the table for Bullant to buy a round of drinks. This didn't stop Buck from continuing to praise his horse and he could see my Dad hated every minute of it. The words were eating into Dad like quick- sand swallowing its victim. With his temper at boiling point and not being able to hold it back any longer, Dad threw out a challenge to Buck. "If you think your horse is good enough, let's race for a quid. Winner takes all. Bullant, you've been blowing your trumpet lately about how good your horse is. Back it up with a quid, that's if you're game enough." Buck knew my Dad's horse could run, yet the thought of winning the money and shutting him up once and for all was too tempting to miss. Buck had put himself in a corner, accept the challenge or shut up. Buck stood up and threw a quid on the table, "You're on," and walked out to the toilet with Bullant following him close behind. My Dad looked at me, "Jumbo, those bastards are up to something."

HORSE RACE

*

Word soon spread around the bar. There was going to be a horse race between the bottleos It caused a buzz amongst the drinkers and they all wanted to be in on the fun. Percy the publican, agreed to start the race outside the hotel and they would race down Nicholson Street and finish at Johnson Street. Dad was not ready to race just yet and bought another round of drinks.

Percy the publican was also in no hurry to start the race; he was doing a brisk trade. More than once, a free beer found its way to Dad's table to delay the race a little longer. The crowd, after waiting for a long time, was now becoming a little impatient and a few drinkers started to wander off. Percy sensed the changing mood of the drinkers and said, "Come on boys, let's start the race." Still cursing each other, Dad and Buck made their way through the crowd of drinkers to their carts, with Bullant following. All three were a little under the weather, as their drinking session had been going on for several hours. The bar was now deserted and everyone was standing outside the hotel. Some were holding their partly filled pots; others were having a bet on their fancy. I was anxious for the race to start. Why was the publican looking further up the road? I then saw a speck in the distance. It slowly grew in size until it became a cable tram. It seemed an eternity before I saw the faces of people sitting in the front carriage, soaking up the afternoon sun. At last, it approached the hotel and came to a stop. The tram driver was wondering what all the excitement was about as he slowly eased the clutch around the underground cable. Then the tram once again became a speck in the distance. The race was now ready to begin. Bullant pulled his horse up beside our cart and Buck was next to Bullant's. Dad said, "Jumbo, sit in the centre of the cart. It's going to be a rough ride and be careful not to fall off." I was tense with excitement as I looked at Percy, who was now holding a white handkerchief above his head. A mighty roar came from the crowd of onlookers when Bullant cut across Dad's horse. While all this was taking place, Buck was off to a flying start and had gained several cart lengths on Dad before he got Darkie, who was now making up the lost ground, into a full gallop. Anything that was lying loose on the cart floor wanted no part in the race. Pieces were flying everywhere. I felt every bump and hole as we raced down Nicholson Street. Buck was belting his horse, trying to get the last effort out of it. Bullant was nowhere to be seen.

The race was coming to an end when Darkie caught up to Buck's horse. For a while we raced neck and neck. Dad was yelling at Buck, calling him all the names under the sun, "Cut me off? You cheating bastard. I'll show you." Then Dad's horse started to lose ground. I guess the effort of catching up was now taking its toll on Darkie. Dad, not to be outdone, picked up the last sack bag, which had somehow managed to stay on the cart. He threw the bag at Buck's horse. This caused it to slow down to a walk. Both the horses were exhausted as they came to a stop. Buck jumped down from the cart cursing Bob, "You cheating bastard." My Dad screamed back, "We both can play your cheating game. Cut me off? I'll punch the daylights out of you." The passing traffic came to a standstill, watching two bottleos putting on a show. Many a Donnybrook they'd had in the past. Usually, it was the soberer of the two that came off best. I was screaming at them to stop and it must have had some effect. They were both in a tight clinch, holding each other up, when Buck said, "Come on Bob, the kid's right. Let's go back to the pub and have a drink with Bullant." It wasn't long after that eventful day that Dad sold Darkie to another bottleo. Dad was like the wind. You didn't know what he was going to do next when he was on a bender.

MY MOTHER

*

My mother was living in a single-fronted cottage in Lennox Street, Richmond with her five children. Dad said she'd had another baby and I had a new brother. I decided to go and see my mother. I didn't really think about why I wanted to see another part of my family. Maybe it was the thought of having a new brother that drove me there, even though there had been next to no contact with that part of the family. I did not tell my Dad where I was going. I arrived at my mother's house a little after lunchtime and hungry. My mother was standing at the front gate with a baby in her arms. My brothers and sisters were playing in the street. Someone must have seen me coming. They stopped and looked at me, not too sure what to do next. Maybe they were waiting for a signal from their mother. I will never know, for I was told to go home as I didn't belong there. I ran all the way back to the hotel to my Dad. I knew he loved me.

My Dad was going to spend time in jail for not behaving himself. It happened one Saturday night when the Black Maria was combing the streets of Fitzroy. He was locked up for resisting arrest. It was now several months since my mother rejected me and I had nowhere to live until Dad came home. I asked my mother once again and she had a change of heart. It didn't worry me living with my new family. I was more concerned with having somewhere to sleep. It must have been hard for my mother to support her six children. She worked full time for SPC Jams in Yarra Street, Collingwood. The company first started making jam in that small factory. The first week, living with my new family, I went shopping with my mother and sister, Shirley. It was raining a little. I was wearing my old overcoat with deep pockets. It was more of a rain coat than an overcoat; it came three-quarters of the way down to my ankles. One day, out bottleoing with my Dad, I found this coat in the rag bag. In more ways than one, it came in very handy. I kept it for a long time.

Walking up Stanley Street, my mother was complaining how hard it was to feed everyone and with me it was going to be a lot harder. I took her words to mean I should shop lift for her. That's what Dad always meant when he was short of money or we didn't have any food. The grocer shop was in Smith Street, Collingwood. It was a big shop with lots of shelves stacked with all sorts of groceries, yet it would be considered a small shop compared with our supermarkets today. While my mother was buying her groceries, I wandered around the shop filling my deep pockets with all sorts of groceries until I couldn't fit any more in. At the counter, I stood beside my mother while her groceries were being checked. I was not a bit ruffled and never thought of being caught. I was pleased with what I had done and started to take the groceries out of my pockets and put them in the pram with the other groceries. My mother said, "Never do that again, you might get caught." "It's easy," I replied, "I do it all the time for my Dad." I was missing my father and didn't like my family much and thought they felt the same about me. I was sent to Cromwell Street State School. I seemed to be in the headmaster's office most days for causing trouble. My stay with my mother only lasted a few weeks before I was on the move once again.

It wasn't as easy as Dad thought it was going to be. When he was released from prison, he came to take me home but my mother wanted me to stay this time. Her boyfriend, the one she ran away with when I was a baby, was now serving time in prison for stealing, so there wouldn't be any trouble with me staying. Unbeknown to me, my mother and father arranged a meeting to decide my fate. I remember that day very well. My mother took me to a single-fronted house in Greaves Street, Fitzroy, just around the corner from my Grandma's place. My Dad had already arrived. He was sitting in the lounge room holding a glass of beer when I entered the room with my mother holding my hand. I was more than pleased to see him, and when he gave me one of his special looks, I just wanted to go over and hug him.

I was told by a man, who seemed to be my mother's friend, to go outside and play while they had a talk. I wasn't too keen to leave my Dad. After a couple of warnings, I left the room. I didn't go outside but hid behind the kitchen door and could hear everything they said. My mother and father were calling each other choice names. They were more interested in themselves than talking about me. When it seemed like Dad was going to fight with the man who told me to go outside, I returned to the lounge room and everything went quiet. Dad beckoned to me to come over and sit next to him. He whispered in my ear, "If you come home with me, I'll buy you a new grey suit and on the way home you can have an ice cream." My mother was looking at us. I think she already knew the answer. The other man said, "Jumbo, your mother and father both want you to live with them, so we decided it would be best if you make up your own mind." There was no need for my father to try and bribe me; I just gave him a big hug. I didn't realise how much I must have hurt my mother. It wasn't until years later that I came to understand she was trying to make up for the time when she deserted me. Feelings of being rejected still sit deeply in me. Not knowing what my problem was when I was young made me fearful and suspicious for fifty years of my life, until I partly worked through it. Dad had moved to a room in Abbotsford. I went to Lithgow St State School, two streets from where we lived for about three weeks. I found it hard to make friends in the school ground. Most kids avoided me when I wanted to join in their games.

I always had this feeling that I was not wanted and it caused me a lot of trouble within myself. A day didn't pass that I was not in the headmaster's office receiving the strap. It got so bad at this school that after three weeks, I was expelled and sent to another school. I think I received more straps in the headmaster's office than I attended days at school.

A ROOM AND ANOTHER SCHOOL

*

Once again, we moved to a room in North Melbourne and I went to Errol St State School. For some reason, I liked this school and settled down a little. For the next few months I was doing very well at Errol Street State School. I was just beginning to understand my school work. Another girl and I had just come top of the grade in the mid-year exams. Our teacher, Mr. Marshall, gave us a speed test before lunch time. The one who was the quickest would win a prize of three pence. Our teacher drew a face of a clock on the blackboard. In the centre of the clock was the number eight. You had to multiply two numbers together, like eight times seven makes fifty-six and so on from one, until you finished at number twelve. The quickest one to do it without making a mistake was the winner. I won the contest. For some reason, I was better than average at arithmetic. Mr. Marshall said, "After lunch we are going to have our first English lesson." Even though I didn't understand what he meant, I was looking forward to it. Over the years, I've often thought of that day, sharing top of the grade, winning the tables contest and losing the chance of having my first English lesson. When I left my classroom at lunchtime, little did I realise what lay ahead of me. I was waiting at the school gate for Dad. He'd said he'd bring me my lunch money as he was working close to the bottle yard. I was hungry, as I'd had nothing to eat except for the bottle of milk I had pinched that morning on my way to school. While waiting for my father, I was eyeing off the kids in the shelter shed eating their sandwiches. I walked over to the shelter shed and bullied the kids and took half a sandwich from them without asking. No wonder I had no friends.

LIFE ON THE ROAD

*

After eating the two sandwiches, I went back to the school gate with my only playmate, Peter and waited for Dad. Suddenly, he appeared with his horse and cart. I said to my mate, "That's my Dad, look at his bottles." When Dad pulled up outside the school gate, he sang out, "Jumbo, do you want to come to the bush with me or stay at school?" At first, I didn't understand. Then he told me he was going to work the bush. "You can come with me or stay with Grandma until I get back. There's good money in fox and rabbit skins." What a question to ask a nine-year-old boy who idolised everything his father said and did! Even the thought of learning could not compete with my Dad. There was nothing in this world that could separate us; I wanted to be with him. I didn't go back to my classroom; it was Dad's way of avoiding the responsibility of having to make a decision.

Little did I know it would be two years later to the day before I returned to another school to sit at a desk facing an English exam paper, which should have happened two years before. I travelled and worked the bush with my father for the next two years with only the odd trip back to Melbourne. Those years played a major part in shaping my life and the moments I shared with Dad still linger in my mind. The times we spent together trapping rabbits, our camp fire chats, the long drives on a moonlit night, begging for food, stealing money, just doing whatever I could to please my Dad, all have a special place in my heart. That's when my Dad was a real dad. I did not go back to my classroom. I jumped on the cart and we drove back to the bottle yard to sell the few bags of bottles and pay Barney seven and sixpence for the hire of the horse and cart. I wonder what Mr. Marshall, my teacher, thought when I went missing. Did he think it was because I'd bullied the kids for a sandwich and was too frightened to face what I had done? If he only knew what had happened, he may have thought differently of me.

Dad was not his usual self. I guessed there was something wrong. It was the same old thing. He had been kicked out of our room for not paying the rent. Once again, a landlord had tossed our few belongings out into the hallway and put a lock on the door. With the little money he had, Dad decided to play cards to see if he could win some extra money. As the afternoon slowly passed by, I could see Dad was losing whatever money he started with.

I thought, if we were going to the bush, I'd better get some money soon or otherwise it would be just another of Dad's dreams.

The few belongings we had were bundled into a couple of sack bags. Leaning up against a bar stool I managed to make a sort of swag, and with that on my back and Dad's hat covering most of my face, I made my way to Coles in Smith Street, Collingwood and sat near the front door rattling my billy. After a couple of hours, I had enough money for our fare to the bush and a bit more. I guess the sight of a little boy dressed up as a swaggie softened many a heart. More than satisfied with the money in my pocket, I made my way back to the Rob Roy Hotel in Fitzroy. It was just on closing time. Dad was leaning against the pub wall with our two bags of belongings, waiting for me. He wasn't too bad; I guess the money had run out. I was pleased to see he was more sober than under the weather. When I handed over a handful of silver and more, a smile came over his face. Walking along Smith Street with Dad, I was carrying the small bag of our things over my shoulder when Dad said, "Are you hungry, Jumbo? We'll have a Chinese meal." We often went to this Chinese café for a meal. I always had the same as Dad, a bowl of short soup and Ki See Min. Sometimes we also had two dim sims. Dad had his funny ways of telling stories when I was eating a dim sim. "It reminded me of the time when we were in Smith Street one day, passing this Chinese shop," Dad said, "See that place? It got caught selling dim sims made from cat meat. They had several dead skinned cats in their fridge."

I believed my Dad, but it never stopped us from eating dim sims. After a satisfying meal, it was now very dark and the air was getting cold. We had to find an empty house. It wasn't hard. We soon found one with the back door wide open at the rear of Smith Street Collingwood. It was a safe place to stay as on either side was a factory. Dad decided to light a fire with the loose weather boards we found hanging from the side of the house. Soon we had a blazing fire going and I was feeling a lot better as I felt the warmth of the fire in the small room. Dad had run out of smokes and said he would go up to Smith Street and buy a packet. I didn't want him to leave the house. I knew he'd wander off with the money and visit the lady in Brunswick Street who ran her business from the front door.

THE LADY IN BRUNSWICK STREET

*

A couple of weeks before, Dad had stopped and talked to her on our way to the pictures. Soon they both disappeared inside. I knew it was on again, so I waited for him. After about an hour, Dad came out. It was too late for the pictures, so we walked down to Ma Maloney's café. To me, it was just as good. Being with my Dad was all I wanted. I didn't want Dad to leave the empty house and wander off and spend the last of our money, so I put on an act, saying I was frightened to stay on my own. Dad let me go and buy the smokes for him. I ran all the way towards the lone light at the end of the lane. It wasn't as easy as I thought to buy Dad some cigs. Smith Street was all in darkness. I knew of a milk bar in Gipps Street, just a couple of streets away. With my packet of cigs, I was soon back at the house, warming myself by the fire. I was very cold when Dad woke me in the early hours of the morning and we both felt stiff and a little sorry for ourselves from sleeping on the hard-wooden floor. The fire had gone out and it was freezing cold as we searched with a lighted match to gather up our few things before we set off to walk into the city to catch a train to Sunbury. There wasn't a star in the sky to be seen.

SECOND WORLD WAR

It was 1940 and Melbourne was like a ghost town at night because of the war. There was not a light to be seen, except for one peeping through a small square in a shop window. The only signs of life were the searchlights scanning the sky, searching for an unidentified plane. I didn't understand what the war was all about, except there were times Dad and I passed two cannons on a wide nature strip in High Street, Clifton Hill. I used to think, "Why are we fighting the war so far away when we have two cannons here?" With these thoughts, once again an eerie feeling filled my body as we made our way along Gertrude Street towards the city. It was about four o'clock when we arrived at Spencer Street Station and we still had a long wait for our train. I was soon fast asleep, curled up next to Dad on the station seat. When he woke me, people were walking and standing close to us. They must have thought we looked a strange sight, eating our bacon and egg sandwich with Dad's hot cup of tea resting on the wooden seat.

I was watching a train as it seemed to twist itself amongst the spaghetti-like tracks. One moment the train was ours, then at the last moment it turned and headed in another direction. All the time I was hoping it was our train. After several near misses I got tired of watching and returned to my seat a little disappointed, thinking, "When will our train come and take us to the bush?"

Then Dad said, "Look Jumbo, there's our train, the one with the red carriages."

I was excited as we finally boarded our train. I sat beside the window and watched the other trains come and go. Ours made its first stop at North Melbourne Station. To my delight, the two passengers sharing our dog box carriage left us. We now had the carriage to ourselves. Dad spread our two bags of belongings on the floor. He was more content to stretch out on the padded seat than to look out the window. It was not long before the train left the city behind and rattled its way to Sunbury. By now, Dad was sound asleep and slept for most of the journey. I think I searched every passing gully and clump of bushes, looking for the movement of a rabbit. We arrived at Sunbury around ten o'clock. "Just one drink, Jumbo," Dad said as we approached a hotel. We stayed at the hotel for the best part of the day until most of the money was gone. Dad had more than enough to drink. Then, for the best part of an hour, we made our way to the campsite. Several times we stopped on the side of the road for a rest. I knew where we were going. Many times, we had camped at this old tin shed when we went rabbiting for the weekend. It was a place where drifting swaggies holed up for a while or stayed longer if there was work around. Darkness was setting in as we approached the shed. I could see the glow of a campfire and three figures sitting around it. I got a whiff of food being cooked. It made me feel very hungry as I'd only had a meat pie back at the township while waiting for Dad. My stomach was all churned up with the thought of food. We must have looked a sorry sight; a man unsteady on his feet carrying a partly filled bag over his shoulders and a little boy walking beside him carrying his lot. We were made most welcome by the swaggies and soon shared a meal with them around the camp fire. Before long I was feeling very sleepy, as the talk around the fire seemed never ending and all I wanted to do was sleep. Dad emptied one of the bags for me to sleep in. I was soon fast asleep in the corner of the shed. I did not realise it at the time, but Dad was not taking any chances. He slept on the outside of me to protect me from the other swaggies, just in case there was any trouble.

Whispers, one of the swaggies, who was to become my favourite as the weeks passed by, was sitting with my Dad when I awoke in the morning. I was very hungry as I watched the other swaggie burn a slice of toast with a long toasting fork. The smell of the burnt toast made my stomach ache from hunger once again. Whispers must have sensed how I felt and got up from his seat and walked over to the shed. My eyes followed him, hoping we might get something for breakfast. A moment later, he emerged with a handful of sausages and a loaf of bread. I watched them sizzle and smelt every drift of flavour that flowed towards me. I thought those snags would never leave the frying pan.

After eating a good breakfast and drinking a mug of hot tea, I helped Dad clear up around the camp and collect firewood. There is a code of honour amongst swaggies. If you arrive at a camp and you are broke and hungry, a meal is always there for you. But if you bludge and do not help around the camp, you are told to move on. Dad got a job filling in rabbit burrows with the farmer on the other side of the hill. He was never afraid of hard work. After a few days working on the pick and shovel, he looked a new man. Working in the open and keeping off the drink agreed with him. With the farmer and Whispers keeping us in food, we survived 'till Friday when Dad got paid. But when the farmer took some of the money for the lunch he'd fed us, Dad got upset and soon an argument started. For once, Dad came off best. The farmer paid all the money and got a black eye for being mean. That was the end of his four-day job. It was the talk of the camp that night and Dad became some sort of a folk hero, gaining respect from the other swaggies. I listened as the night grew colder. Dad told them how he had fought at the Fitzroy Stadium and taken on all comers. He didn't say anything about being drunk and fighting for ten bob when he was desperate for a drink. The next morning, Dad and I walked into town and the little money he had for his few days' work soon went on beer. Now we had no food, so my half-drunk father said I should do my old trick, knocking on house doors and asking for something to eat. It was something I'd done before.

DOOR KNOCKING FOR FOOD

*

I knocked on the first door and asked for some tea and sugar, giving the excuse that we'd just arrived in town and Dad had no money till he started work the next day. Dad waited around the corner for me to take whatever I collected. Then I went to another house and asked for some bread. I repeated this many times, collecting food. People were kind to me; wanting to give me a bowl of sweets or take me indoors and sit me at the kitchen table. I had a keen eye. Over the years, I became good at lifting things. My eyes searched the room for any loose money that might be lying around. If I had a chance, I would take a little, always remembering what Dad had taught me, "Take a little, and leave a little." I always felt pleased when I did those sorts of things for Dad, as I knew he would be pleased with me. It seemed although we'd come to the bush to make money trapping rabbits, Dad was not a bit interested in rabbit skins. He was more contented in the bush, filling in rabbit burrows for a farmer when he felt like it and spending whatever money we had. His moods with the drink were less frequent, apart from a couple of times when he got into an argument at the hotel. Meanwhile, with the food we were providing at the camp, Dad and I became very popular with the other swaggies. I must have kept the camp in food for weeks. When Dad was drinking in the pub, Whispers came with me and waited around the corner, just like Dad. I was now enjoying my life at the camp, although winter had well and truly set in and at night it was cold sleeping on the hard ground in my sack bag. The couple of blankets Dad managed to get from a farmer weren't enough to keep out the damp air. There was never any thought of taking my clothes off, they were a permanent part of me. For several weeks now, we had been at the camp. There was a steady stream of swaggies drifting through the hut. Some stayed a night, others a little longer. They all seemed to be going nowhere, just drifting. I was a lot wiser now with grown men and now and then a swaggie tried to get too friendly if we were alone together. But I was once trapped into going into the shed by a newcomer. I was lucky to get away. I pretended to go all quiet, then I saw my chance. I managed to get out of the shed. He never bothered to come after me and I ran all the way into town to tell Dad. He was drunk, so I decided to wait until he sobered up. Later that night when we got back to the camp, that swaggie had packed up and left. I was glad as I didn't want my Dad to get hurt if he had a fight.

MY FRIEND WHISPERS

*

It was another one of those days. I had just finished begging for food with Whispers, and we had nearly a good half bag of assorted food. There was enough to last the camp for a week. I said to Whispers, "I want to go and see my Dad," not telling him I wanted to give Dad some money I'd swiped from a lady's kitchen when she'd left me alone for a few minutes to pick some fresh vegetables for me. I left Whispers at the corner and watched him disappear down the road and for a moment I thought, "Why can't Dad be like Whispers?"

LIGHT FINGERS

*

Back at the hotel, I was sitting with my Dad who was playing cards, when a man walked in and straight away shouted drinks for everyone. Dad said to me, "He must be a local as everyone seems to know him." The man was telling one of the drinkers in a loud voice he had just arrived home from a shearing run where he had made a lot of money. He began to throw his money around as if it had gone out of fashion. Meanwhile, Dad was watching him and as the afternoon wore on, Dad made his move. The shearer was now leaning on the bar to support himself and was very drunk. His drinking mate had gone home. Dad whispered, "Jumbo, go over and sit beside him and see if you can pick his pocket."

I had been watching him and his money too. I went over and sat right next to him and started to talk. He put his hand in his pocket and pulled out a handful of notes and bought me a drink. It was too easy. I slipped my fingers into his trousers pocket and pulled out a small bundle of notes. I sat with him for a while, biding my time, then casually wandered to the toilet. Dad followed me a little later and I gave him the money - four pounds. I felt pretty proud of myself when Dad ruffled my hair and said, "Smart boy Jumbo, I am proud to be your father." I felt as big as a mountain. He gave me a couple of bob for some lollies and told me to get back to the camp before the shearer missed his money.

Whispers was all alone when I arrived at the camp. The first thing he asked was, "Are you hungry, me boy?" I didn't have to say much. I just sat down by the fire and watched my friend cook me a well-earned meal. "Where's your Dad? I guess he's at the pub." I didn't answer. The whole camp knew he couldn't keep away from the drink. I loved these moments being with Whispers, when we sat around the campfire together. He liked to tell me a story like the one he told as we waited for the billy to boil. He said one day he was out trapping rabbits when he came across a gully where they were so thick, he had to push them away to set the trap. I couldn't understand why he didn't grab the rabbits instead of setting the trap. That was Whispers, always pulling my leg. It was getting dark and Dad had not returned from the pub. Whispers could see I was getting worried and said, "Come on Jumbo, let's go for a walk along the road and meet your Dad." We had been walking about a mile when I saw a figure staggering along the track. I was so glad to see my father that I ran the last hundred yards as fast as I could. All Dad said was, "Where have you been, Jumbo? I was waiting for you."

TWO NEWCOMERS

*

Later that evening, we were all sitting around the campfire when we heard voices in the dark. For a moment, we all stopped talking and waited. Two swaggies appeared out of the dark. Whispers said to me in a soft voice, "They're new ones on the road. Look at the way they are carrying their swag. They don't even know how to roll their blanket into a tight roll." One was carrying a suitcase. This put a smile on the other swaggies' faces. They were made welcome by Whispers who seemed to know what to do. He saw to it they had a mug of hot tea and a slice of toast.

Swaggies depended a lot on each other for news along the track. These two had very little to tell, as it was their first time on the road. They'd been looking for work in the town to no avail and were going to spend the night by the creek when a passing farmer told them about our camp. The two newcomers were not the only ones looking for work. The Depression had been over for a few years now, but it had still left its mark on the unskilled worker. That's one of the reasons why there were so many men on the road looking for work. The camp was now full and everyone was in a happy mood except Dad. He seemed to resent the two newcomers as if they were invading his territory. He didn't take part in the camp talk. I could see he was going to put on a scene. Meanwhile, Whispers was telling the two new arrivals how some farmers wouldn't give you the time of day. All swaggies had a code of practice for warning others to keep clear of certain farms. If a farmer was mean, four small stones were placed near the farmer's gate, a sign not to go in. If you saw three stones, it was all right to go in. You might get a meal for chopping a week's supply of wood or maybe an odd job or two.

While all this fire talk was going on, Old Joe, who had been at the camp for over a month, was very quiet. At night, he made things to sell in town. He was an expert at making gadgets from fencing wire he stole from the farmers. He made soap shakers from tobacco tins, billies from powered milk tins and toasting forks by the dozen. It was his way of making ends meet and to keep his pipe filled with tobacco. There was another swaggie at the camp and on the odd mornings if Dad was not going to work, sometimes I helped him to pick bits of wool from the barbed wire fences where the sheep rubbed against the fence. We always came back to the camp with a half bag of wool. When the swaggie had enough wool, he was off to town to sell it to the wool buyer. Sometimes he did this twice a week. I think he made more money than anyone else at the camp.

A LAZY SWAGGIE

*

As the night was coming to a close, Dad still hadn't said a word. I could see he was in a rotten mood. When he got like this, he would pick a fight over nothing. It was only a matter of time before he picked on someone. Finally, he started on the swaggie who'd arrived two days earlier. Whispers had already told him if he didn't pull his weight, he had better move on. He was very lazy and that very morning, Dad had told him to get off his arse and get some firewood. Dad began calling him all the lazy bastards under the sun. The swaggie ignored him, just kept looking into the fire, playing with the last of the red coals. But then Dad went too far and the man rushed at Dad, swinging his fists. The other swaggies grabbed both of them until they quietened down. Next morning the swaggie packed his swag and left. We stayed at the camp for another two weeks, then Dad decided to move on to another shed. I was missing Whispers as we spent so much time together when Dad was at the pub. I think there was a time in his life when he had a family of his own. We packed our few belongings and made our way towards Melbourne. Several times I looked back and saw Whispers waving to me, then I lost sight of him and never saw him again. Dad was not sure what he wanted to do. I think his mind was made up for him when we got a lift to Melton. He knew of a tin shed just out of the town on the bank of the Werribee River where swaggies camped. We received the usual welcome and soon settled in. Here life repeated itself, with us surviving the best way we knew how. I was expecting Dad at any moment to say, "I've had enough, let's go back to Melbourne where I can make a decent quid," but to my surprise he said one morning, " Pack up Jumbo we're going to Bacchus March, I can get work on the vegetable farms."

The next morning, we left the camp; as the saying goes, we hit the road and managed to get a ride most of the way, arriving at Bacchus Marsh just after lunch. It was mid-afternoon before a goods train was due. "Just a couple of drinks Jumbo." Two hours later we were back at the railway siding waiting for the goods train. I got excited when I heard a train whistle as we hid behind the goods shed and were soon lost in an avalanche of steam as the train came slowly to a halt. At the right moment, we threw our things into an empty cattle truck and scrambled aboard. It was really exciting lying amongst the bales of straw, listening to the sound of the whistle as it approached the railway crossing. The continuing clutter clatter of the train wheels was soothing and I didn't want it to end. I watched the passing countryside through the wooden slats. Then the train slowed to a crawl as it started its climb up Werribee Gorge, helped by another steam engine that had joined it at the bottom of the climb. The train finally made it to the top and started to gather speed. Dad opened the sliding door and threw our things onto the side of the track. We then jumped into a clump of grass without hurting ourselves.

TIN SHED

*

Regaining my thoughts, I stood for a moment and watched the train disappear under a cloud of steam behind the ridge. Dad had already picked up our swag and was pointing towards a creek at the bottom of the steep incline. I could barely see the tin shed from the top of the ridge. I thought it was about half a mile to the camp, a lot better than walking four miles or so by road. It was close on sunset when we arrived at the hut. We were in luck as there were two swaggies sitting by the fire. One was from our last camp and he warmly greeted us with a meal. The tin shed was built around 1935 for workmen who did maintenance work on the lock, which controlled the irrigation water. Then there was no use for the shed, and it became a place for swaggies to camp for the night until it was demolished.

A LIFE SAVER

*

The irrigation channel that was carved out from the hills of the Werribee Gorge in the days of the Depression ran for several kilometres till it reached the lock. A few hundred metres from the lock the channel crossed three gullies supported by three wooden structures which had long ago served their purpose like the running water. Now only the ruins of the channel tell you it was once a life saver for those who were lucky enough to join the suso queue for ten shillings a day that provided a meal for hundreds of men and their families during the days of the Depression. All the work was done with pick and shovel, day in and day out. I was enjoying my time at the camp. If only Whiskers were here, it would be complete. We had just about everything we needed. In the valley, there were many vegetable farms. In exchange for a little work, we could have all the vegetables we wanted, or at night we went down and stole a cabbage or two. There was a dairy farm not far from the hut. I soon got to know the farmer and before long I was getting up early in the mornings and helping him with the milking. Every morning, the farmer milked fourteen Friesians by hand. Sometimes I'd help put the cows into the milking bails and put hay in their feed bins to keep them quiet while they were being milked. After a few tries, I became very good at milking and the farmer must have taken a liking to me. When we'd finished milking the cows, he'd take me back to the house and we'd have a breakfast of bacon and eggs.

I also helped the farmer to separate the milk. While I turned the handle, I would watch that I didn't go too fast and spill any milk over the side. The farmer fed the pigs with the skim milk and while he was doing this, I'd collect the eggs for the farmer's wife. A couple of eggs were left in the long grass for me to take back to the camp. Some days the farmer's wife gave me lunch. Not once did I ever think of stealing from them, except for a few eggs. It was better than living in Melbourne. I always felt warm in the house, not like the rooms we lived in, or the tin shed. I was even allowed to have a bath and the farmer's wife gave me some old clothes

TO WEAR WHILE SHE WASHED MINE

*

Back at the camp, if we wanted a fresh rabbit for stew, there were days I helped Sawn off Tommy set several snares when we found a fresh tear or two in the wire fence. We always caught more rabbits than we needed. Sawn off Tommy was a little man, barely five feet tall. One night, we were all sitting around the campfire doing our usual thing when my Dad said to Tommy, "Why don't you go into town and sue the council?" Tommy wasn't too sure what Dad meant. He said, "What for?" Dad burst into laughter, "For building the road too close to your arse." Then the swaggies laughed. Poor Tommy got up from the fire and went straight to the hut without saying a word. I felt sorry for him, as I knew what it was like to be ridiculed, even in fun. Dad began working at one of the small farms, doing odd jobs for a woman. I didn't take much notice of her at first. It was only when Dad began coming home late at night that I took more notice. She was different to the other women in Dad's life; she didn't drink beer and didn't talk much. When she went into town to do her shopping, she would bring back beer for Dad.

A NEW WOMAN

*

It was the talk in camp about the woman living on her own. I think the other swaggies were jealous of Dad. It didn't worry me Dad had another woman. I knew it wouldn't last very long. I was happy at the camp knowing Dad wouldn't be drunk every day. There were only the three of us at the camp now, Tommy, Dad and me. The others had decided it was time to move on. With Dad coming home late most nights, Tommy and I fended for ourselves. I thought Tommy was like Whispers, sort of looking after me, but one afternoon he showed me his penis and tried to get me to sit on his knee. I ran down the track and fetched Dad. Tommy tried to cut across the paddock when he saw Dad running towards him. There was a fight and we left the swaggie in the paddock, wishing he hadn't tried to touch me. I was proud of my Dad the way he protected me. Dad didn't go back to the woman's place that night. We had tea and spent the evening together around the campfire. Things were going fine at the camp. Dad had his woman and was spending less time in the pub. I was spending all my time between the two farms, helping with the milking in the morning and later in the day I'd go to the other farm and help Dad. Some days we stayed and had tea at the lady's place. I didn't like her very much; she seemed to resent me. We were the only ones now staying at the camp. We would light a fire and fry a rabbit for our tea. With the warmth of the fire fighting the cold night air, I waited for Dad to tell me a story. Tonight, it was about catching rabbits. Dad started talking about rabbit skins. "They are bringing a good price Jumbo. We should set ourselves up and catch rabbits here. It's not too late, the winter isn't over yet." Dad carried on about making rabbits nets and getting a couple of ferrets. "We could make good money." My thoughts were always the same, "Will it ever happen?"

DADS ULCER

*

A few days after our talk about catching rabbits and selling their skins, Dad woke up with a pain in his stomach. The pain was worse than usual. "Jumbo, my ulcer is giving me hell. Get me a glass of water and my antacid powder." After a little while, Dad knew he was in trouble because the medicine had no effect. He decided to break camp and head back to Melbourne before his ulcer burst. I ran to the farmer's house to tell him Dad was sick and we were leaving. I think he was sort of sorry to see me leave. The farmer said I was a good kid and I should go to school. How right he was.

We packed our few clothes in a hessian bag and left the rest of our things in the hut. Maybe they might come in handy for a desperate swaggie. It was midday when Dad called into the farmhouse and said goodbye to his woman and told her he was coming back when he got his ulcer fixed up. I knew that wouldn't happen; tomorrow was just another day to Dad. It took us just on an hour to walk into Bacchus Marsh. I was feeling hot and tired from the long walk. Dad didn't want to stop at the pub for a drink; his ulcer was giving him hell. Instead, we bought a bottle of milk and I ate a pie as we sat on a seat in the main street of the town. We started walking along the Avenue of Honour towards Melbourne and every now and again we sat by the roadside for Dad to have a rest. We started walking again, then Dad tried to wave a car down, but it just kept going. The ulcer was giving him hell, so much he could hardly walk . Dad had given up trying to get a lift. The next time we sat down, a driver must have felt sorry for us sitting by the side of the road and stopped the car next to where we were sitting. He popped his head out of the car window and said, "Are you alright mate? Do you want a lift to Melbourne?" It felt so good sitting in a car. I kept looking out of the window, hoping to pass a car I saw in the distance. The driver could see what I was thinking. He said, "We'll never be first to Melbourne. There's always another car ahead of us." With these words, I slipped back in my seat for the rest of the journey. Everything came and went at such a fast pace; we were in Melbourne before I realised. The man insisted on driving Dad to the house where I was going to stay until Dad was better again.

I have lived in many a dump but I think this was the worst house I ever saw. The front fence had completely fallen down, and the verandah spouting was hanging by its last thread. I noticed the dirty, torn curtains hanging over the window ledge. The window had been smashed and all the broken glass was scattered on the verandah. I waved goodbye to the man in the car as Dad knocked on the front door. There was no answer, and this time Dad gave the door a real thump with his fist. He swore when he heard footsteps in the passage, "The lazy bitch's been asleep." An enormous, overweight woman appeared, with a scraggy- haired girl clutching her dirty apron. Her snotty nose was firmly fixed on her top lip. Every now and again, she would run her tongue over the snot. The stench from inside the house was paralysing. We had arrived at Dirty Flo's place. How Dad knew where she lived, I never asked. The last time we were living in Melbourne, Dirty Flo lived in Collingwood. Flo was pleased to see Dad. She gave him a hug and said, "How is my little baby? I would have my little girl here on one breast and you on the other." It was not the first time I had heard this story. In years to come, I often wondered whether this snotty –nosed girl was my half-sister.

But Dirty Flo's mood seemed to change when Dad told her he was going to the hospital to have his ulcer checked and asked if she would mind me for a few days. We had little money and Dirty Flo wasn't happy about feeding an extra mouth. When Dad left to go to the hospital, he said he was feeling a lot better and would catch the bus. Dirty Flo kept telling me I should find somewhere to live, so I asked if I could take the pram in the backyard and use it to collect beer bottles to make a little money for her. That cheered her up and the next morning I pushed the pram down to Fitzroy and worked the back lanes close to the bottle yard. My Dad had taught me to do this when you didn't have any money and you wanted to sell the bottles quickly. Several times I loaded the pram and returned to the bottle yard. By lunch time I had made a few shillings. If I was lucky, I bought a battery or a copper bath heater. As my Dad would say when he made a good deal, "Jumbo, that call made my day." I was soon building up a good bank for my Dad. Each day Dirty Flo ask me how much I'd made. I would put my hand in my pocket and take out the money and give it to her. Two or three shillings. Whatever else I made, maybe another four or five shillings, I hid in the pram for my Dad.

HOSPITAL

*

Meanwhile, Dad had been admitted and operated on and every afternoon I saw him at the Royal Melbourne Hospital and gave him the money and told him how I worked the back lanes. If I had got a good deal, he would ask me about it, "That's not the way I taught you." Then he would tell me what I had done wrong. I lived for my Dad. I could feel a glow of pride flowing from my body as we talked. Dad was full of new ideas when I visited him. "Jumbo, when I get better, I'll stay off the booze and save some money for a horse and cart before we head back to the bush." I would agree with him, knowing all the time it was impossible for my Dad to save some money. There were times when Dad did own a horse and cart for a short time, but it was like everything else. He sold it for a drink.

After three weeks in hospital, Dad was still not fully recovered from his ulcer. I had not missed a day in seeing him. The only other person to visit Dad was Grandma. It was me who'd told her he was in hospital. I'd gone to her house one afternoon and she took me inside and gave me a bath and told me to stay there while she went down the street. When she came back, she had a bundle of new clothes for me. The day I arrived at the hospital in the new clothes, Grandma was there and she told Dad he should be ashamed for letting me look like someone dragged up in the gutters.

One rainy morning I decided it was too wet to go and collect bottles in the pram. Instead, I stayed home, trying to keep out of Dirty Flo's way. I was sitting on the floor next to the open fireplace, playing with the fire when it happened. Dirty Flo was boiling clothes in a four-gallon kerosene tin on the open fire when I disturbed something. The tin slipped off the crossbar and came tumbling towards me. The boiling water spilled over my body and legs before I had a chance to move. I jumped up, screaming for Dirty Flo to help me. She came into the room and seemed more concerned about her washing than me. She started to pick up the remains of the clothes from the floor and put them back into the kerosene tin, while I was jumping up and down screaming with pain. She screamed at me to shut up. I tried to take off my shirt to ease the pain. The clothes had stuck to my skin. Dirty Flo wasn't a bit interested in my burns. She said I was a sook and would be glad when my Dad came out of hospital. I had enough sense to know I had to go to hospital as quickly as I could. I walked a few hundred yards to Lyon Street to the bus stop. Every step I took seemed to take a piece of flesh from my body. I told the conductor I had no money and a tin of boiling water had spilled over me and I had burnt myself. "I want to go to the hospital." He seemed to understand and let me ride for free. I remember the bus was crowded. People were pressing against my burns with every movement of the bus. My pain was almost unbearable.

When I reached the Children's Hospital, I didn't know where to go. There seemed to be people everywhere. Then I saw a nurse and showed her my burns. My clothes had become a part of my body. I was admitted straight away and put on a trolley and wheeled into the operating room. I woke up and found myself in a ward with other children. It was a strange feeling being so close to them. I was unsure of myself without my Dad. All my clothes had been taken off me. I lay naked under a large cage which kept the sheets from touching my burns. A small light was shining under the covers, which I think was to keep me warm. My body and legs were covered in a blue dye. This was constantly sprayed on my body to ease the pain. The hospital wanted to know where I lived. I said my Dad was in the Royal Melbourne Hospital and I did not know where I lived as we just came down from the bush. Slowly, a thick brown scab appeared, covering my whole body and the top part of my legs. The hospital got in touch with Dad and the next day he walked out of the hospital and came to visit me. I liked being in hospital. Dad never missed a day to see me. He always bought me lollies. I was moved out to the balcony for the last part of my stay in hospital. There was a brick wall and a garden close to the bed. When the horse and cart turned into the street, I could just see Dad for a moment, then the cart disappeared. When Dad parked the cart up on the footpath, his face just appeared above the brick, having the cart on the footpath. Then Dad would throw me a bag of boiled lollies. He was a good shot as the lollies landed close to my bed or sometimes on the bed.

In the bed next to me was a girl about my age who wanted to share my lollies. I wasn't too keen and only gave her one when I felt like it. She wasn't satisfied with a few lollies and said she would tell the nurse about my lollies. After that threat, I had to share them with her. For the several weeks I was in hospital, the only other person to come and see me was Grandma. Meanwhile, Dad had rented a house down by the river, close to the Yarra Falls Woollen Mills and was living back with Violet. I didn't really mind as I liked Violet and when I left the hospital, she looked after me while I was recovering from my burns. As for the house, it was a big old weatherboard with a front and side verandah. From the back yard I could see the bamboo sticks on the other side of the river bank that hid the secret cave I had found one morning when I was playing amongst them. The cave was part of the river bank and high enough to stand up in. It became a part of my life for many years to come. The back yard of the house was long and wide and it gradually followed the deep embankment down to the river. It was a paradise for a boy to play in. I made myself a sled from an old piece of roofing tin with one end turned up to rest my feet against. To keep my balance, I held onto two pieces of rope tied to the tin. A thousand times I must have gone down that embankment, just stopping at the edge of the river. When I wanted to play amongst the bamboo sticks, I had to walk down the street and cross the bluestone bridge. One morning, I saw two boys paddling a tin boat down the river. It gave me the idea of making my own little boat out of a sheet of corrugated iron and tarring the ends to make it waterproof. I could cross the river instead of walking round. I thought I was very smart the first day I paddled my little boat across the river, even though I couldn't swim. It didn't occur to me the little tin boat could sink. Dad was still the same, having good days with the drink and bad ones, like fighting with Violet. I was happy with myself; I had the river and my secret cave. School was a thing of the past; we had lost all contact with the man in the grey suit. Christmas came and went without any fuss. Then Dad started coming home from the pub in a raging mood. I think he was in some sort of trouble and poor Violet got the worst of his outbursts.

One day, when she'd had enough, she packed her few things and left once again. We didn't go to work the next morning. Dad told me to stay home while he went and collected the horse and cart. When he returned, it wasn't the same horse and cart from the bottle yard. I asked him where he'd got it from and he just said, "I borrowed it for a while." I still thought we were going to work when Dad said, "Jumbo, we're selling up and going bush." For the rest of the day we loaded pieces of furniture and anything of value, including my bike, and sold the lot to the Smith Street Auction Rooms. The same day, we packed the last of our belongings, including a tarpaulin to cover our things on the cart if it rained. I was sorry to leave the house. I loved my playground and the river, my little tin boat and my sled; no one was going to have my boat or sled. I punctured a hole in my little boat and watched it slowly drift away while my sled sank to the bottom of the Yarra River. Little did we both realise, as we drove away in the early hours of the morning, this trip would be the last time Dad and I would spend together in the bush.

THE LAST TIME TOGETHER

It was just on daybreak when we arrived at Keillor and made camp by the creek. Dad decided to stay a few days and work the township as we could sell our scrap close by. We then moved on to Clarkefield and camped at the bluestone stables behind the hotel. I wasn't happy about going to Clarkfield as I knew what it was going to be like being so close to the hotel. There were two swaggies camping in one of the stables; Dad and I had the other one. It wasn't too bad except for the cobblestones when I slept at night.

After a week of drinking, Dad decided to move on and for the next two or three weeks, we travelled and camped on the side of the road. Sometimes we pulled into a swaggie's camp and stayed until Dad decided it was time to move on. I was always looking out for Whispers or asking had anyone heard of him in their travels, but to no avail. We survived by working the farms and selling our scrap. I did my usual stunt when needed, begging for food. Life on the road with my Dad was good. For many days, we did very well. On one farm, we nearly loaded the cart with old coppers and brass fittings. Dad wouldn't touch batteries as they were too heavy and of little value if carted for a long distance. I was disappointed at first; thinking if I had them in Melbourne, they would be the talk of the pub with the other bottleos. But the satisfied smile on Dad's face was enough for me to forget about the batteries.

We were close to Ballarat. Dad wanted to reach the town before the weekend so he could sell his load. I knew we had a good load worth several pounds or more. On our way into Ballarat, we passed a deserted farmhouse and by the look of it, nobody had lived there for a long time. You could hardly see the house as it was overgrown with weeds and grass. We pulled up outside the front gate. I wanted to have a look inside. Dad said we didn't have time and would come back later to look it over; it might be the place to stay while we scrapped the town. We arrived at Ballarat on the Friday afternoon and soon found a scrap dealer who bought our load. The money was burning a hole in Dad's pocket; it had been a while since his last drink. While he sat in the pub, I roamed around the town spending a little money on things that took my fancy. I was walking down the main street when I saw a lot of boys and girls. Some were with their mothers going into a picture theatre. I couldn't read what the large sign said, but I liked the look of the boy with the long nose. It was Pinocchio and I walked out of the theatre feeling sorry for the old man, as I thought Pinocchio wasn't nice to him. It was starting to drizzle as I helped Dad onto the cart, but I didn't mind. It had been his first drink for a while and I'd had a great time exploring the town. Dad had already covered himself up and was starting to snore his head off. His last words as I was bending down at the back of the cart trying to light the hurricane lamp were, "Find a dry spot, Jumbo."

FARM HOUSE

*

I remembered the old farmhouse as I drove the horse and cart down the main street of Ballarat. The rain was now starting to come down a lot heavier and it was beating down on Dad's face. I covered him with the tarpaulin and tried to protect myself with a bag around my shoulders. It wasn't long before I reached the farmhouse. There was a large tree overhanging the front fence. I managed to drive the horse underneath the branches to protect us from the rain. I sat for a while thinking about what I should do. The sound of Dad snoring was tempting me to cuddle up to him. But I was wet and so was Dad, so I decided to get down from the cart and have a look inside the house. I walked around to the back of the cart and unhooked the hurricane lamp. The front gate was overgrown with thick grass. I managed to climb over the top and I was now completely wet from the long grass. The light from the lamp flickered against the house wall as I fought my way along the broken path. It was a ghostly feeling, passing one after another broken window pane. I didn't know what to expect next. Every time I took a step, the sound of water squelched from my shoes. The bracken was so thick I seemed to be lost in my own jungle. As I flashed the light in a different direction to find a way through, it picked up a small break, just big enough for me to squeeze through, and I found myself on the back verandah. Most of the floorboards were missing, so I stepped carefully between the rotten supports as I made my way to the back door. I tried the door handle and pushed. The hinges made a loud squeaking noise, sending a chill up my spine. I hesitated for a moment and thought of Dad lying on the cart. But the drive inside me to please him overcame any fear that I might have had.

I thrust the lamp through the half-open door and the light flickered along the passage wall, catching a sort of wreath. I stood in my tracks and froze for a moment, the flickering of the hurricane lamp against the wreath sending another cold feeling through me. I decided to get out of there and get Dad. I retreated onto the verandah and the thick bracken, but the thought of getting soaked again made me return to the back door and gather my senses. I had been in the dark before in an empty house and nothing had happened.

This thought gave me the courage I needed to venture down the passageway, at the same time avoiding eye contact with the wreath. I found myself in another room. Except for an old couch in front of the open fireplace, the room was empty. I guessed this must be the lounge room and then wandered back to the passage and found myself standing at the front door. I pulled back the steel bolt and turned the brass knob without much effort and the door opened. A cold wind cut through my wet clothes as I fought my way again through the wet long grass and climbed over the broken gate to the cart. Dad was still sound asleep and I had a devil of a time waking him up. I decided to unharness and feed the horse with the last of the chaff, then went back to the cart and managed to wake Dad and tell him we were at the empty house. When we got inside, Dad didn't care where he was, he just collapsed on the old couch. I covered him up with a blanket and found a bed in one of the bedrooms. I seemed to have full control over my Dad in these sorts of situations. When he was sober, he was my Dad and when he was drunk and beyond thinking, I am sure now I took the place of his Dad, who he'd never known. Dad was an early bird. He lit a fire in the open fireplace and I was woken by the smell of a breakfast being cooked. I was starving. Dad was crouching over the fire making toast and he must have heard me stir because he said without looking up, "This will be a good place to stay Jumbo, until we get kicked out."

It had been a long time since we'd had a proper roof over our heads and it would be a change to sleep in the bed we found in one of the bedrooms. We worked all day making the house comfortable; we found several pieces of furniture in a shed overgrown with bracken. One piece was a kitchen table. Our next job was to fix up the fencing in the back paddock so we could keep the horse in. It was not going to be that easy as we had no tools, only a shovel which I'd picked up from a farm when the farmer wasn't looking. My Dad was good at fixing things and soon we had a small section of the paddock for the horse. By the end of the day, the house looked as if someone was living there. We stayed there for some time. Dad seemed to be more contented than he had been for a long time and he wasn't drinking as much, just every now and then he would get drunk. After a day's work, he was happy to come home and do odd jobs around the house.

BALLARAT

*

We were doing very well in Ballarat, collecting from just about every house we door-knocked. Dad said, "This place hasn't been touched in years, we'll make a packet here." We were living like kings. There was always plenty of food and things to eat. I had never seen Dad like this before. When he was away from his mates, beer didn't seem to worry him like it did in Melbourne. This life seemed too good to be true and I wondered how long it would last, as I knew any day Dad would find a woman and go back to his old ways. Dad had seen an advertisement in the local paper for three dozen rabbit traps for sale and said they would come in handy for the winter time. We went to the address and were standing together on the verandah, waiting for the door to open, when a young woman appeared from the side of the house. Dad asked her about the rabbit traps. I could see from the way Dad was talking he was more interested in her than the traps. This spelt trouble for me. Then he forgot about the traps and asked her if she had any scrap to sell. I was told to stay and watch the horse while they disappeared down the backyard.

Some time went by. I was getting anxious. Dad had been gone a lot longer than he should have. So, I got down from the cart and followed the path that lead to the back door. Here was Dad sitting at the table drinking a glass of beer with this woman. I knocked on the fly wire door with a look of disapproval on my face. The lady, without moving from the table said, "Come in." But I continued to stand at the door, looking at Dad. He knew what I was thinking. He said, "This is my right-hand man," and told me to load the rabbit traps and wait for him on the cart. I was wild to think a few rabbit traps were going to set Dad off on another binge. I was thinking about driving the horse back to the house when Dad appeared with the woman and told me to take the horse and cart back home. I was so mad I took my anger out on the horse, hitting him as hard as I could with the reins. The poor horse was in a lather of perspiration when I arrived at the house.

Later that evening, I heard the sound of a car pulling up at the house. It was Dad in a taxi, together with the woman and a load of beer. It was the start of another bender and I soon learnt this woman liked the drink as much as Dad. They drank and stayed in bed for days. Slowly all the hard-earned money disappeared on drink. Dad was back to his old ways. I escaped these drinking sessions by spending my time looking for birds' nests or shooting at anything that moved. I know now I was taking this rejection out on the poor birds or anything that got in my way. Besides my Dad I had no friends and when he had a woman in tow, my own company was all I had. I consoled myself with the thought, "It won't last forever, especially when Dad starts to give her a belting or two." Before long, my prayers were answered. A feeling of satisfaction came over me while I was watching Dad hit her. Irene, that was her name, got up from the floor and never said a word but gave Dad a look as if she could kill him, went into the bedroom and gathered up her few things and walked out the front door, holding her face. Dad followed her out onto the road, calling her a good-for-nothing slut. That was the last I saw of her.

I was glad she was gone. Now I wanted to leave the house and hit the road, just in case she came back. I didn't want to lose my Dad again. But as Christmas approached, it became obvious Dad had no intention of moving. He was working in the mornings and drinking every day with a couple of men he'd teamed up with. Some days, Dad and his mates came back to the house and drank into the late hours of the night. Then two weeks before Christmas, Dad decided to dry out and get rid of his hangers-on. On the Friday before Christmas, we sold what metal we had and did some shopping. It felt good to walk around with my Dad once again. I was a good shopper for my age. Dad was far too impatient, so he gave me some money while he sat on the cart and waited for me. I wanted to surprise my Dad and give him a present for Christmas. I was in a shop that sold all sorts of things and came across a cut-throat razor on a shelf. I looked around and then when nobody was looking; I slipped the razor into my pocket and walked out of the shop. I expected to see Dad waiting for me. I was surprised to find no sign of him. It didn't take much to figure out where he was. The temptation of a hotel a few doors from where the cart was parked had been too much for him. I walked into the hotel and there he was, playing cards with his glass of beer beside him. It was going to be a long afternoon and I didn't want to hang around waiting for the pub to close.

Before I left, Dad gave me a handful of pound notes to mind. This pleased me. I knew this wasn't going to be the start of another bender and drove the horse at a slow trot back to the farm. I wasn't in any hurry; I had all the afternoon to fill in. Brownie seemed pleased when I let him loose in the small paddock. He kept running around in a circle, kicking out his two back legs as if he was saying, "Thank goodness I am free of the harness." I was now feeling hungry and lit a small fire in the kitchen stove and cooked myself a couple of eggs on toast and two chops. It was still mid-afternoon and to fill in the time while I waited for Dad, I did my usual thing, hunting with my shanghai.

I was on the back porch skinning a rabbit when I heard Dad sing out, "Jumbo, come and give me a hand." I left the half -skinned rabbit hanging on the three-inch nail and found Dad standing by a taxi door, fumbling in his pockets for change to pay the fare. On the ground were three parcels of beer in brown paper bags. I bent down and picked them up and gave one to Dad. By the look of him, two more drinks and he would not have made it home.

We managed to make it to the front door and he collapsed on the lounge room couch. I went back and finished skinning the rabbit, then washed it clean of blood before soaking it in a pot of salted water. For the rest of the night, Dad didn't move from the couch. I left him there and went to bed, remembering that the next day was Christmas Day.

CHRISTMAS DAY

*

The sun was shining brightly through the broken window as I lay awake soaking up the warmth of the sun. I listened to a magpie calling its mate. For a moment there was a pause, then I heard the calling sound of another magpie. I imagined they were both flying to a tree top to build their nest. The sound of Dad moving around the house woke me from my dreamy thoughts. The smell of bacon drifted through as I made my way to the kitchen. A drop of vinegar in a chipped glass was on the kitchen table surrounded by broken egg shell. I guessed Dad's hangover was worse than usual. I ate my breakfast in silence. Dad would never talk much while he had a hangover and I knew from past experience to tread lightly until mid-morning.

Dad was starting to be more talkative by the time he started to cook the Christmas dinner. It was the chance I had been waiting for all morning and I gave him the razor. I didn't bother to wrap it; I just wanted to give it to him. He was really pleased, then looked shame-faced and said he was sorry but he hadn't had time to buy me a present, but when the shops opened, he would. I didn't care. All I wanted was Dad to be my Dad. It felt like one of those Sundays when we were in Melbourne. Dad cooked a terrific Christmas dinner; roast lamb, roast potatoes and a bread-and-butter custard. I could not remember the last time we had such a good meal. I was pleased the pubs would not be open and even though there were still several bottles of beer left, Dad was not in the mood to drink. We finished dinner, I helped Dad to clean the kitchen table and waited for him to say, "Jumbo, how about a game of crib?" I rushed into the bedroom and carried the box with the well-worn cards to the kitchen table. Dad had taught me a lot of different card games and for the next part of the afternoon, we played several games of crib and grabs.

When Dad took a short nap, I kept playing with the cards, building them on top of each other until the whole pack was standing on edge. Many times, when I was just about to place the last card on the stack, all the cards would come tumbling down. I would get so mad with the cards, then think of the story my teacher had told me when I was in the third grade about Robert the Bruce and the spider. I tried again, pretending I was the spider, until all the cards were on their edge. That evening, we played crib again by the light of a candle and the hurricane lamp hanging over the kitchen table. I went to bed that night with a feeling I never wanted to lose. For the next week, Dad and I never left the house. We did odd jobs and were just father and son to each other.

Toward the end of the week, when we were clearing grass around the front fence, a flash car pulled up at the house. A well-dressed man walked over to Dad and said, "I'm the owner of this place. Are you living here?" Dad was never short of words when he was in a tight situation. His method was to attack. He was straight to the point. "The bloody place was empty and deserted. We'd been on the road for three months, my boy was very sick and as we were passing by, it was raining cats and dogs. My boy was all wet and I knew if I didn't get him shelter, he could finish up with double pneumonia. I only intended to stay the night. The next day I made inquiries in the town to see if I could rent the place if I cleaned it up. Nobody seemed to know who owned it. But you can see for yourself how we've worked on the place." The man's wife got out of the car and said, "What a sad story. Is that your boy?" "Yes, lady. Three weeks ago, you would not have thought he was the same boy, he's put on so much weight." I think the owner was impressed with the work we had done and the way Dad talked. When he asked to have a look inside the house, Dad and I kept working to make a good impression while they decided our fate. I wasn't too worried. The house was clean, and there wasn't much for them to see except a kitchen table and two wooden chairs, plus a built-in cupboard which Dad had made out of old wooden boxes. In the lounge room was the open fireplace, with the burnt ashes still smouldering from the fire we'd had the previous night. The old couch, with its sunken springs relying on the wooden floorboards for support, was the only piece of furniture in the room. Then there were our beds, a double and a single, and our few clothes hanging from a makeshift hanger.

But deep down, I was hoping they would tell us to go. I still thought Dad's woman might come back. When they reappeared, they were both smiling.? They crossed over to where we were working and the man said, "You've got no right to take possession of someone else's house, no matter how bad a condition it's in but seeing you've done wonders to the place, you can stay on and pay a small rent if you continue to keep the place tidy. How's that?" Dad agreed to pay rent and said he would send a payment to Melbourne as soon as he went back to work. They shook hands and we both waved goodbye and I watched their car disappear towards Melbourne. But I knew Dad had no intention of sending any money and a month later we were on the road again, first cleaning out everything of value. Dad took out the cast-iron stove, leaving a gaping hole in the kitchen wall, the copper from the laundry, the plaster wreath and anything else we could sell in town. I felt a little sad as we drove away from the house; except for the woman, I'd enjoyed my stay. The horse was fresh and in good condition for a long trip.

STAWELL

*

Dad decided to make for Stawell. If he kept off the drink, everything would be all right. Along the way, we worked the farms on the main roads, being selective in what we picked up, as we knew we could not sell until we reached Stawell. At one farm, Dad was doing a deal with the farmer, so I wandered into a large shed where I saw a big stack of chaff bags. I knew they were worth a couple of shillings each, so I loaded several dozen, covered them up with the tarp and sat innocently on the cart.

When the farmer walked off to work on a water tank, I told Dad about the bags. He was not pleased with me. "Jumbo, we are not in Melbourne. This is the bush and we could get caught on the road if the farmer misses them." He shook his head, "Jumbo, you will get me shot. Let's get out of here as fast as we can." As we drove down the track, the farmer waved for us to stop and started to walk over to the cart. Dad said, "I don't like the look of this," and jumped off the cart so the farmer couldn't come too close to it. Ironically, the farmer asked if we bought chaff bags. Dad always had a quick answer when he was in a tight corner. "Yes," he said, "but we don't have room now. But in about a fortnight we'll be back around this way and will call in."

The farmer seemed satisfied and waved as we drove through the double gate. He was still waving when he closed it after us. Life on the road was good. The weather was holding and soon it would be autumn, but the horse was starting to get tired, so Dad decided to make camp next to a creek and rest for a couple of days. We had managed to pick up a tent at one of the farms and more rabbit traps. It was a lot better than sleeping under the cart at night.

We reached Stawell on the Sunday with an extra passenger. The day before, a drifter had stayed the night and told us he was heading for a shed about a mile out from Stawell. He said it was a good place to stay, with plenty of fresh water. The farmer who owned the shed was a good bloke and never refused you a bit of grub in return for chopping a week's supply of wood.

We arrived at the camp and received the usual welcome from the swaggies already camped there. It was a large tin shed, more than enough room for us. But when two swaggies started eyeing our load of metal, Dad walked over to them and said, "Keep your eyes off the cart, or there'll be trouble." That night, Dad decided not to sleep in the shed, and we made our bed under the cart to protect our things. The next morning, Dad said we were leaving. "Why?" "Those two thieving bastards. I wouldn't trust them as far as I could throw them. Not every swaggie on the road has good intentions."

We found another place not far from town. Later that morning, we drove into Stawell and found a buyer for our load. Unfortunately, he was the only one in Stawell and the price was low. Dad was furious. "The cheating bastard, I'll get even with him for taking me down." With several pounds in his pocket, Dad made for the pub and soon found a card game. I went off on my own and bought some food and returned to the camp, only to find the swaggie we had picked up two days earlier sitting on a log waiting for us. He wanted to know where my father was. I said he'd be back soon and unharnessed the horse, making sure he wouldn't wander off. Then I hid the rest of the money a little away from the camp. By now I was starting to feel nervous of the swaggie and when he said, "Why don't you come into the tent and have a rest?" I ran down the track and onto the main road, where I hid in the bushes for a while. Later I saw the swaggie walking in the other direction, so I returned to the camp and got my shanghai and hunted some rabbits while I waited for Dad.

When I returned to the camp with three rabbits, Dad was nowhere to be seen. The fire was still smouldering from the warm ashes; it didn't take much to restart it with dry twigs. I then cooked myself a sausage and toast for my tea. It started to get dark and I suddenly had a feeling Dad was somewhere close by, lying on the side of the road. I had only walked a few hundred yards and there he was, too drunk to move any further. He was sleeping it off. I tried to wake him. All I could get out of him was, "Where have you been, Jumbo?" It was his favourite saying when he was drunk. I must have heard it a thousand times. That was my Dad, always relying on me when he was drunk.

It took another week for Dad to come out of his bender. Each day, about five o'clock, I'd wander up to the hotel and somehow get him back to the camp without him getting into some sort of fight. Slowly, the money dwindled away. This never worried me and in my own way, I was glad to see it all go. I knew my Dad would be sober for the next few days. We were soon back to our old tricks; me begging for food and stealing whatever money I could lay my hands on.

Then Dad was offered a job collecting bottles for the dealer at so much a dozen and whatever scrap he picked up was his own. Dad thought it was a good deal and decided to give it a try. He still had it at the back of his mind to get even though, because the dealer cheated him on every scrap metal deal. Yet the dealer was also pleased with the number of bottles we were collecting, not that Dad ever paid much for them, his motto being, "Put the bottles on the cart first and pay later."

One morning we came back to the yard with a big load. The dealer was waiting for Dad and called him aside. Apparently, the local policeman, who was a friend of the dealer, had told him to tell Dad to call into the police station. Dad went into the station while I waited with the cart around the corner. The authorities were concerned I wasn't going to school and it was suggested I could stay with the dealer's family and go to school instead of sleeping in a shed with swaggies. I was not happy about leaving Dad, even though he said it's only for a week or two before we make our way to Sunbury for the winter.

A STRANGE FEELING

*

It was a strange feeling sitting at the table with these people, eating my tea. Once again, I couldn't manage the meat and the dealer's wife, seeing I was having trouble, cut it for me. There were two other children at the table, both about my age, a boy and a girl. I could see they were sniggering to each other. I felt like punching them in the nose and the table cloth frightened me once again. I thought at any moment I was going to spill my food and make a mess. All I could think of as I stared at my meal, was sitting around the campfire with my Dad, eating from a tin plate using my fingers and no one would care if I dropped my food in the dirt.

I had to get away from these people. I was so relieved when I left the table and was told to have a hot bath and was given a clean pair of pyjamas to wear. For the next hour we all sat in the lounge room and I was asked about my life on the road and did I have a mother. I didn't say much and soon they got tired of asking me questions. The dealer's wife showed me where I was to sleep and said good night as she closed the door. I didn't like the feel of the pyjamas, nor the sheets. For the past few months my clothes had been my pyjamas and a sack bag my bed on the ground. Thinking this was not for me, I quickly changed back into my old clothes and jumped out the window, running all the way through town to the camp. Dad didn't growl at me when I said I wanted to be with him and didn't like staying with the dealer and his family. The next morning, Dad woke me from a deep sleep and was ready to leave the camp. It was too risky to stay another day in Stawell. If I didn't go to school, I could be taken away as a neglected child.

ON THE ROAD

*

After resting the horse every few miles, we reached the outskirts of Ararat. Dad soon found a good spot near the creek for a campsite. For the next two days, we rested the horse and just lounged around the camp. Dad wanted to move to the next town as soon as possible because he was not too sure if it was safe to stay here much longer. On the road again, the first day we just took it steady with the horse and made camp for the night. The next morning, Dad talked about trapping rabbits and what we needed. This excited me. At last we are going to make a lot of money. When we reached the next town, we made camp on the outskirts.

"I want to go too," I said. "I don't want to be left at the camp all by myself." "I'll be back on the afternoon train, promise," Dad said. "I want you to stay behind and look after the horse and the camp."

The next morning, we arrived at the station with two bags half full of metal. Soon the train arrived and we loaded the metal into the guards' van. I thought it would fetch us quite a bit of money and never doubted Dad's word when he said he would come straight back. Dad told me more than once I shouldn't wander too far from the camp and if any one came, to tell them I was just going to meet my father. I understood what he meant. When the train came into view, I gave my Dad a hug and promised to look after the horse, then waved him off. "See you tomorrow, Jumbo," he called out. It was to be the longest week I think I ever spent. Every day I went down to meet the train only to be disappointed with the same sad feeling. I kept busy though, taking the horse and cart and doing my own scrapping, going from house to house, picking up whatever scrap I could. I did what Dad had taught me to do. I would say I hadn't any money to pay for the scrap and people gave me things. I suppose it must have seemed strange, to see a boy, I was ten nearly eleven, driving a horse and cart around the streets, collecting scrap and begging for food. I had gathered an assortment of things and I think I was trying too hard to please him. What I should have been thinking was to shoot him for leaving me all on my own in the bush for a week.

One day, I was standing outside the front door of a house asking for food when the lady told me to wait a moment while she went to the kitchen to get me a sweet. I could hear the sound of voices and the smell of a roast made me think what it would be like to live in a house with a family of my own. Maybe it was for the best that Dad went to Melbourne. I think I was beginning to grow up and understand there are better things in life than begging for food.

When Saturday came, I thought Dad must be on the train because the next one was not till Monday. I was over-anxious and thought the train had come and gone when I saw only two people waiting for it. Then more people began to arrive. I saw a woman struggling with two suitcases. I must have looked a poor kid to her in my ragged clothes and with my disheveled appearance. The woman stopped, "Could you help me onto the train with one of the suitcases?" I jumped up from the seat and lifted the case without much effort and she smiled at me. "My, you are a strong little man," she said. I told her how I'd been coming down to the station every day to meet my Dad and how I was staying at the camp by myself. She was a nice lady. It was the first time I had talked about myself and it felt good to have someone to listen to me. She wanted to know all about my life on the road and by the time the train arrived she said I must love my Dad very much and he must be a good father.

I heard the train whistle blow twice in the distance and I could see the smoke blowing freely as the engine appeared around the bend. It seemed like an eternity for the train to reach the station. My heart started to race as I helped the lady with the cases. I was in a hurry so I would not miss my Dad. The train finally came to a standstill and I opened the train door and quickly pushed the cases between two seats and waved goodbye to the lady. Then I ran along the platform looking for my Dad. There was no sign of him. I was now sure he hadn't come. But a few stragglers were approaching the gate where the stationmaster was waiting to collect tickets and that's when I saw Dad walking toward me. Violet was a few paces behind, carrying a small suitcase with her handbag tucked under her other arm, trying her best to keep up to Dad. I ran towards him and gave him a big hug. I forgot all about saying hello to Violet. I was so excited to have my Dad back. All he said was, "I'm a bit late, Jumbo." I didn't care, my first words to my Dad were, "You should see all the scrap I got for you". "Good boy Jumbo." It made me feel good even though he was a week late. I had forgotten all about Violet in my excitement of being with Dad again. Violet came forward and tried to kiss me on the cheek. I pulled back, blaming her for my Dad being late. Yet I really knew why my Dad hadn't kept his promise to return the next day. His weakness had once again got the better of him. Dad didn't talk much. He seemed tired when we arrived back at the camp. I wanted to know if he had any money. I was asking all the questions, how much money he'd got for the scrap metal and how much he had left. Stupid questions. His binge with Violet had taken all the money except for the train fare.

The next morning, the three of us were sitting around the campfire talking about what we should do. I was right about Dad having spent all the money. We had little food and there was no way we could sell the scrap I'd collected locally, so Dad decided to break camp and make for the next town.

BALLARAT

*

I did not realise, as we left the town, it was the last time I would beg for food. I was starting to find it a lot harder to beg. I knew I was blushing and I felt hot and bothered. Meanwhile, I began to feel better about Violet's presence. Of all the women Dad had brought home, I liked her the best. She always stood up to Dad and had a happy knack of quietening him when he was in one of his outrageous moods.

Dad was starting to be concerned about the weight on the cart; the horse had slowed down to a walk. Once we camped for two nights and a day to give the horse a rest. After what seemed like a never-ending trip, we arrived on the outskirts of Ballarat and made camp. It was a good place for fresh water and well-sheltered from the wind. Dad was good at finding the right place to pitch a tent. The next morning, Violet stayed at the camp while Dad and I went into town and sold whatever I collected to the scrap dealer. A couple of hours later, we returned with fresh supplies. Dad decided to have a break from the drink and work the town so he could build up a bank for the coming winter. Dad was serious about working hard. Each morning we set off early and returned to the camp about lunch time. Violet stayed at the camp and had the fire burning and a billy of hot water waiting for Dad to have his wash. The camp was nice and tidy and, by the time we had finished around the campfire, we had made plans for our trip to Sunbury. After so long in the one spot, Dad was getting anxious to move on. It was good to see Dad like this. Little did I know it was to be the last leg of our journey together.

SUNBURY

*

From Ballarat we made our way to Sunbury. Dad was not a bit interested in scrapping now, for he'd made enough money over the past weeks to last us till we sold our first lot of rabbit skins. He said if we stayed there for three months, we would make money from the skins to set us up. He was well prepared for the winter. We had managed to pick up several dozen more rabbit traps, three ferrets with nets and another small tent.

When we arrived at the township of Sunbury, we bought whatever we needed for the first week, then made camp four miles out from the town on the road to Riddle. It was a good place for a campsite. Just inside the wire fence was a large well. From the dirt road it just looked as if someone had built a round brick wall about three-foot-high with a tin roof, but when you opened the wooden door, you heard a deafening roar of water gushing through the underground tunnel on its way to Sunbury to fill the township taps.

Inside the well were several iron steps that descended to the bottom where you could stand on a small wooden platform. Many times, I lowered myself down these steps to the platform to keep our food cold. One slip and I would have been sucked through the tunnel to finish up in a hundred taps in Sunbury. This was really a dangerous thing for a boy to do. Not once did my Dad ever venture down. There were times I opened the well door more than once a day.

Dad got the idea if he placed two thick wooden poles across the top of the bricks, we could hang several dozen pairs of rabbits above the swirling water. Dad passed the rabbits to me and I supported myself with one hand while I leaned over the rushing water, trying to put more rabbits on the poles.

The big tent Dad used for himself and Violet. The small one was used for keeping our food and other things we needed daily. At night, I slept in my sack bag on a mattress the same as Dad. The camp was nearly the perfect spot. We had everything we needed compared to what we had when we left Melbourne. But there was one big drawback, the wind. It seemed to blow a gale every day. When I got up in the morning, I didn't want to venture out of the tent; it was so strong and biting my face felt like an ice block. Just a few hundred yards above the camp was a dairy farm. The farmer was pleased Dad was going to trap rabbits on his property. He gave us two ferrets and nets. This meant we now had five ferrets, which was ideal, as we could rest them every second day. He also let Dad put the horse in the paddock next to the well. I soon became friendly with the farmer and every morning after we came back from resetting the traps, I made my way up the hill to the dairy, swinging the billy over my shoulder and pretending it was full of milk. I even felt quite pleased with myself that I hadn't spilt any. The farmer was very generous to us and once gave us a six-week-old poddy calf which Dad killed and skinned. We lived on fresh veal for the next week.

It was hard work trapping. Late in the afternoon we'd set forty rabbit traps, then about nine o'clock at night we checked them for any rabbits we'd caught. The cold wind. It seemed to cut me to pieces as I stood holding the hurricane lamp while Dad collected the rabbits and reset the traps. Dad slit each rabbit's throat to drain the blood, then take the innards out. To save time and extra hard work, we'd hang pairs of rabbits on a fence and collect them the next morning. At daybreak we'd be out in the hills, facing the chilling wind, checking the traps. If we didn't have the horse to carry the rabbits and the traps, our work would have been a lot harder. Violet was always up and waiting for us when we arrived back at the camp with our catch. The fire was alight and a billy of boiling water was waiting for Dad to have a warm wash before breakfast. I did not realise it at the time, when Dad went to Melbourne to sell the metal and he left me to fend for myself, it was Violet he wanted. Without Violet to look after us, I think we may not have lasted a month at the camp. I am sure my life would have gone in a different direction. My last job for the morning was to help Dad skin the rabbits and peg the skins on wires. The three-quarter grown ones we kept for the rabbit buyer who passed the camp every second day. It was ready cash, which we hadn't expected.

When we finished our work, Dad and Violet retired to the big tent and slept until lunch time. I guess I had too much energy for a sleep; I always found something to do to fill in my spare time. I was loving the life at the camp even though it was a hard life.
Meanwhile, we were attracting attention and a family living in a tent and in such poor conditions, a little boy not going to school and the washing strung along the farmer's fence for every passer-by to see.

We had now been at the camp for some time and although Dad was not drinking as much; we went into town each Saturday. Violet and Dad spent the afternoon in the pub while I waited for them. It was on one of these trips Dad heard talk about me not going to school. I think he sensed there could be trouble and said I was not to go to town anymore. Our hard work was now starting to be worthwhile. We had collected several hundred skins and Dad was undecided whether or not to break camp because of the gossip and head back to Melbourne or stay on a little while longer. In the end, he decided to send me to Melbourne to sell a bag of skins, as we were just about out of money.

Dad and Violet drove me to the Sunbury station to catch the morning train. As usual, the wind was blowing a gale and it was bitingly cold. Our poor horse had suffered in the paddock with no protection from the wind; I could see he'd lost a lot of weight because his ribs were showing. This time, it was my turn to say goodbye. The station master let me ride in the guards' van with my bag of rabbit skins. I looked out of the small window and waved to Dad as the train pulled out of the station. I heard his last words, "Don't forget to catch the five o'clock train back tonight." I enjoyed the train trip. The guard knew all about me by the time we reached Melbourne. I had great pleasure in telling him how we had been on the road and now were trapping rabbits, and I had caught two white ones and kept them as pets in the wire cage Dad made for me. He was a kind man. I didn't have anything to eat and he shared his lunch with me. I arrived at Spencer Street Station before twelve o'clock. Just a few hundred yards from the station was a big brick building and a sign in large letters, Haughton Skin Buyers. I had been there with Dad several times before, selling our skins. It was a bit of a struggle to carry the sack bag of skins; I had to put it down several times and drag it along the ground. Before we left the camp, Dad told me I should get about seven and sixpence a pound for them, according to an article he'd read in The Age.

When I arrived at the store, a man appeared and carried the bag to a set of scales. I watched the scales closely. I then asked the man how much a pound for the skins and he said five shillings. "My Dad said they are worth seven and sixpence a pound," I said, and showed the man The Age article. Eventually, I was paid the right price of thirty pounds. Even though I'd had very little schooling, sums were my strong point and my dealings on the cart had been something that all the schooling in the world couldn't have taught me. I still had the rest of the day to fill in before I caught the evening train back to the camp, so I walked along Bourke Street thinking about the thirty pounds. Several times I put my hand in my trousers pocket to feel the notes. I bought myself something to eat and soon found myself outside the Lyceum Theatre in Burke street where a large bill board was on display showing two men fighting with swords. I couldn't read all the main words, but it looked good to me. When it finished, I saw it again and was puzzled about how someone could get killed and still be alive when I'd just seen him die. I was so mixed up the second time I forgot all about catching the train and stayed to see it for the third time.

It was dark and I was hungry when I walked out of the theatre and then it hit me, I had missed the train. I stopped at a cafe and had a hot meal of steak and eggs. I wasn't a bit worried as I walked up Little Bourke Street to Gordon House. For a shilling I had a bed for the night. The next morning, I caught the train back to Sunbury, hoping Dad would be at the station to meet the train. There was no sign of Dad and I walked the four miles to the camp, and for a moment I thought no one was there as it was all quiet and it felt deserted. I looked in the tent and there were Dad and Violet, sound asleep.

Dad wasn't a bit concerned that I was late. He was more interested in how much money I'd got for the skins. I gave him the money and I knew I had done a good job. That same afternoon, we all went into town to get supplies. It was getting dark when we finally walked out of the hotel. Dad was a little under the weather and Violet wasn't much better. People were staring at us as we drove away from the pub. Dad was swearing at Violet and was starting to get nasty. Then in her own way, she had quietened him down by the time we reached the camp. Our horse was now too weak to carry the traps. The winter and cold winds were taking their toll. In Melbourne, Dad had always taken great pride in looking after his horse, but here at the camp he'd just left it in the paddock to fend for itself. I made another trip to Melbourne to sell more rabbit skins. I managed to get a ride to the station with Harry, who bought our rabbits and was now bringing our supplies to the camp. Dad was now more content to have his drink and stay at the camp with Violet. This time, I made sure I did not miss the evening train. I went to the same theatre and saw The Man in the Iron Mask, then made my way back to the station to wait for the train. While I was away, our horse died and Dad had skinned the horse and was pegging out the skin when I arrived back at the camp. I gave him the money and after having my tea, we set out to collect the rabbits from the traps. It was a lot harder without the horse; we had to make three trips back to the camp carrying rabbits. The next morning, we had to do it again and that was the last time I ever went trapping with Dad.

A WARNING

*

We were pegging out the skins when the farmer appeared, saying he thought he should come and warn Dad. The town and school committee had a joint meeting about us living in a tent and a young boy not going to school. The committee decided something should be done about the family with the small boy. The farmer said he'd just had a phone call from the local police station and the sergeant wanted to know if we were at the camp as he was coming up with an officer from the Education Department. Apparently, there was a warrant to take me away. My Dad quickly decided I should leave the camp and go to Melbourne. As we were standing outside the tent saying goodbye, I saw a motorbike and sidecar in the distance slowly climbing and winding its way towards us, leaving a cloud of dust in its wake. A policeman was driving the motorbike, his helmet reflecting against the sun as if to signal me to run. The other man was sitting in the sidecar. Dad said they will be here in a matter of minutes. He told me to walk down to the creek and follow it for a couple of miles, then follow the train line to Digger's Rest station. I will never understand why. We had money from the rabbit skins, but Dad made me carry the wet horse skin eight miles across the paddocks and hills to Digger's Rest Station. I had to stop for a rest often and many times I was going to throw the horse skin away; it was heavy and my arms felt as if they were going to fall off. I finally made it to the township and was relieved to sit on the station seat and wait for the afternoon train.

Dad didn't give me any extra money apart from two shillings for my fare. He said the money from the horse skin was more than enough till I got to Grandma's place. I arrived in Melbourne just before the skin store closed. For all my effort in carrying the skin across the hills, I was paid the sum of six shillings. I had not eaten for several hours. The first thing I did was buy myself a pie and a small bottle of milk.

ARRIVING AT GRANDMA'S

*

I was not too sure about going to my Grandma's. I was trying to think where else could I go and thought about my mother. Would she want me after the last time when I refused to go with her? For the next couple of hours, I wandered around the city streets until it got dark. I finally made an effort and caught the tram to Grandma's place. I nervously knocked on the front door, hoping Grandma would open it. I had to knock a second time; a lot louder. This time, a man opened it. I had seen him before when Dad and I had visited Grandma. "What do you want?" he asked. I tried to explain Dad had sent me, that we had been trapping rabbits at Sunbury for several weeks and a policeman was going to take me away for not going to school. I was left standing at the door for several minutes while my fate was being decided. The same man came back and asked me to follow him down the dark narrow passageway and to wait at the bottom of the staircase. I could hear voices in the kitchen discussing what should be done with me. When another voice said I should stay the night until Ma came home the next day, I realised

Grandma was not home and I was in the hands of these people who did not like my Dad. Even though I'd had nothing to do with her, I knew my sister was in the kitchen. I could hear talking. She said, "We don't want him here." Those words have rung in my ears for the past seventy-eight years.

I was told to come into the kitchen. My sister was about fifteen years old at the time and you would think I was the devil the way she looked at me. I was allowed to stay the night and sleep on the lounge room couch. I didn't sleep much; I was too scared I might wet the couch. When I wanted to go to the toilet, I sneaked out the front door and urinated in the gutter. This wetting the bed didn't happen very often now, but it was always on my mind when I went to bed. I thought about my Dad and when was he going to come and get me.

It was about mid-morning the next day when Grandma arrived home. I was in the backyard with Donny Russell, one of Grandma's boarders, talking about Dad, when Grandma appeared. I told Grandma what had happened at the camp and that Dad sent me to her. Grandma asked a few questions and how Dad was, then said I must have a bath. I was told to sit on a chair in the backyard and have my hair washed with kerosene. "Disgusting," my Grandma kept repeating as she ran the fine-tooth comb through my hair to clear the dead lice. My head was so infected, Grandma decided to get her friend Donny to cut most of my hair off. I had several large sores on my legs and feet and my socks were firmly stuck to them. It was too painful for me to remove them, so I had to soak my legs in the bath to take my socks off. Then Grandma gave me a good scrubbing and asked me when was the last time I'd had a bath. "I can't remember," I said, "I think it was when I was in hospital." All my clothes were thrown away and new ones were bought for me. It was a beautiful feeling to be so clean.

Grandma lived in a lovely, two -storey house. The iron picket fence and the Victorian lace work, which seemed to smother the whole front of the house, made it stand out from the other houses in the street. The Hawthorn bricks and the lost art of tuck-pointing that had remained intact, added to the beauty. It wasn't a large house compared to the other houses in the street. There was a bedroom, a lounge room and a long passageway which seemed to take up all the space. A very small kitchen was at the end of the house. Upstairs was a large balcony room and a small bedroom. Halfway up the staircase was a landing, with a door that led to a small room divided into two by a small partition, which made room for a bath with a wood heater on one side and a bed for one of the boarders on the other.

My Uncle George arrived home on the Sunday night from a

shooting trip with his fiancée, Phyllis, and wanted to know what I was doing sitting at the kitchen table. Grandma said it was her home and she would do whatever she wanted to do. My Grandma ran her home with an iron fist. Her word was never questioned and this gave me the protection I needed. Eight people lived in that over crowded house and with me now there were nine. There were three male boarders, one a cousin to Grandma who I was told to call Uncle Jack, he was a veteran of the first and second wars, George Crapper, a friend of the family who went home to Bendigo most weekends and Donny, who was old enough to be my father and seemed to be Grandma's favourite. Donny took me under his wing and gave me his support. Then there was my sister, June who was five years older than me, a total stranger and treated me that way and Uncle George, who disliked me because I was his brother's child.

Within a few days of arriving at Grandma's house, I enrolled myself at George Street State School, just two streets from Grandma's place. The year was 1942. I was eleven and a half years old and because of my age I was put in the fifth grade, even though I had less than fifteen months schooling. It was just on two years since I last went to school and I remembered that morning like it was yesterday. We were going to have our first English lesson after lunch, but my Dad came to school at lunch time and took me away. Now two years later, on my first day back at another school, an English exam paper was put in front of me.

I was not ready to tackle an exam paper. I was seated with a boy who, for some reason, seemed to enjoy pinching my leg. I told him to stop it more than once. This made him pinch my leg again. After more pinching I had had enough and without any warning, I gave him a black eye. The teacher came over to where I was half -standing and dragged me out of my desk by my shirt collar. I felt I was being choked by his tight grip as he rough handled me all the way down the stairs to the headmaster's office. I was given a good talking to and two straps for hitting the boy.

I was then taken back, with threats from the teacher, that next time he would do it himself and I was lucky to get off so lightly. I was also put at a desk by myself in the front row of the class. My exam paper was waiting for me to do something instead of just staring at it. Finally, I did and made a complete mess of it. I was more than pleased to hear the school bell ring for morning recess. Making my way down the first flight of stairs with the other children from my class, a boy jumped me from behind and started to punch my back. Children scattered everywhere. I retaliated and was marched off to the headmaster's office once again. This time I was given a real dressing down and received several straps for something I didn't start. The headmaster didn't believe me when I said I was pushed and punched in the back. It was still playtime, so I went straight out and saw the kid who pushed me. Across the road from the school is a laneway with another one running off the side. We settled our differences after a couple of minutes. The kid said, "I've had enough," and we both walked back to the school ground as if nothing had happened. In due time, that kid Ken Rushgrove and I became the best of friends. After recess, I was still struggling with the exam paper. My teacher asked me to stay back after school. I told him I travelled with my Dad in the bush and hadn't been to school for the past two years and how I had come to live with my Grandma. After our talk, my teacher took a personal interest in me and helped a lot with my homework. George Street State School, like other schools in the nineteen thirties and the forties, had their problems in the playground at recess times. The playground was controlled by a school bully and his mates. Because of what had happened in the morning, it was all over the school ground, the new kid was going to fight the school bully. I was sitting by myself eating my lunch when three kids approached me. One was the kid who had given me trouble on the stairs earlier, the other two were the school bully, Victor and his mate. Things were different in my day. If there was trouble, it was one on one. The kids sat in a big circle and watched the fight. I looked up at the window on the second floor and saw several teachers watching. Not one teacher made any attempt to come down and stop the fight. The boy I had to fight was from the sixth grade and a lot bigger than me. The sight of an Aboriginal put the wind up me a little. In later years, these two kids, Vic Lovett and Ken Rushgrove, became main event fighters at Festival Hall Stadium in West Melbourne. I easily won the fight. Victor went home with his brother before the lunch time bell rang. I was standing in line with other kids waiting to go to my classroom and expecting any moment to be dragged off to the headmaster's office. Instead, my teacher came to me and said, "I'm glad you gave that kid a beating. He's been looking for it for a long time." After my first day at school, I settled down and had no more trouble. Three weeks later, Victor came back to school. I was ready for the unexpected. It never happened.

I kept out of Uncle George's way if we were alone. He more than once ran my Dad down and told me how lucky I was he allowed me to live in Grandma's house. His fiancée Phyllis came from Ballarat to live with Grandma. Her mother was a lifelong friend of Grandma, they'd both once lived and gone to school together in a small town called Creswick a few miles from Ballarat, it was a sort of arrangement that one day George and Phyllis would get married, but there was never a greater mismatch between two people, unfortunately for dear Phyllis. For twenty years or more, they lived in the same house and were engaged for most of that time. Because the house had only three bedrooms and a closed in balcony to sleep nine people, Phyllis slept in the same bed as Grandma. I wonder would it happen today, sharing your double bed with your future daughter-in-law for all those years?

I shared the balcony room with Uncle Jack and Donny and was always dreading the nights. The thought of wetting the bed was always on my mind. Maybe it was the white bed sheets that helped me never to wet the bed again. Uncle George slept out on the balcony. At night when going to bed, he would have to climb through the balcony window as part of the balcony room. This arrangement lasted for over thirty years. Even though Donny was old enough to be my father, we became best of mates. On a Tuesday night, we sometimes went to the Regent Theatre in Johnson Street, Fitzroy, to see a picture and at interval Donny would buy me an ice cream and a packet of lollies. When Donny came home from work on a Friday night, he'd give me two shillings pocket money and tell me not to say a word about it. My other two uncles never gave me a thought. The two shillings stopped when I finished school and got a job, but he still shouted me to the flicks. On hot summer nights, Grandma, Donny and I caught a bus to St Kilda beach. Grandma and I sometimes watched Donny swim a long way out to sea. At times he disappeared among the rolling waves and Grandma would stand up and watch out for him to appear again, unable to keep her eyes off Donny's powerful strokes. A smile would come over her face and she'd say to me, "Isn't Donny a wonderful swimmer?" I was not a good swimmer, I could barely dog paddle, so I was content to let the small waves tease my feet. When Donny had finished his swim, he would run back to where we were sitting and dry himself. While I was playing with my sand castle, I looked at Donny's muscles and wondered if I'd be like that one day, then look at my pigeon chest. Uncle George was always telling me my chest was deformed or like a girl's chest. Donny also liked to go off for a run along the beach and suddenly appear with three ice creams and a bottle of soft drink and when we'd finished our treat, he'd help me build my sandcastle. This is what I will always remember about Donny. He was so generous and always doing the unexpected.

Then, when it was time for Grandma to gather our things, the three of us walked to the pier to collect mussels. I carried a gunny bag and waded out with Donny until the water reached my waist, while he would swim a little further out to the deep water, fill his bag with the mussels that clung to the pylons, then swim back to where I was standing and pour them into my bag. It wasn't long before my bag was sinking to the bottom of the sea from the weight of the mussels.

When we arrived home, I would help Donny light the wood copper in the backyard and cook the mussels. When the shells opened, they were the colour of an over-ripe mango. We'd pick the seaweed from the mussels, then put them in milk bottles and seal the top with greaseproof paper and a rubber band.

Donny could do no wrong in Grandma's eyes. He liked his drink on a Friday after work and if he came home under the weather, Grandma would tell him off and threaten to kick him out. It never happened. His tea was kept warm in the wood oven and then he wandered off to bed. I was waiting to follow him upstairs and take his shoes off and ask him if he was all right. He just looked at me with his funny grin and fell asleep.

Unfortunately, there was always tension amongst the men in Grandma's house. The British United Shoe Machinery Company of Australia, where the three men worked, was in Alexandra Parade, Fitzroy, not far from Grandma's place. Uncle George worked in the office as paymaster, Uncle Jack in the tack room and Donny was a knife-maker.

Living at my Grandma's and going to school on a regular basis began to make a better person of me. Uncle George, ensuring I would not be a burden, went out of his way to get me a part-time job in Kerr Street, Fitzroy. After school, I worked one and a half hours every day, and all-day Saturday, nailing four pieces of wood together to make one end of a banana box. My pay was a ha'penny for each one I made. I averaged one pound and four shillings a week. My pay was sealed in an envelope. Thursday after work, I gave my pay to Grandma unopened. She seemed contented to have me around and for the next eighteen months I never missed a day at school and seldom at work. I more than paid my way.

Although several months had passed since I'd left the camp, Dad never bothered to come and see if I'd arrived safely at Grandma's. I had no idea if he was still in the bush or back in Melbourne. Then one night I was taken by surprise. I was playing quoits on the front verandah when I heard his voice, "Jumbo, are you coming home with me?" The front door was slightly ajar. Grandma had told me if Dad came to the house and he was drunk, I was to come straight inside and close the door. But Dad was already standing near the gate, blocking me from going into the house. I could see he was drunk by the way he held onto the iron gate.

Then Grandma saw Dad from the front window, where she was sitting at her sewing machine making aprons. She told me to go inside and then I heard her say to Dad, "Get the hell out of here! Jumbo is not leaving. Come back when you're sober." I went to Grandma's bedroom and peeped out from behind the curtain in time to see Dad stagger away from the house. I didn't feel anything for him at that moment. There had been a time when I would have run out of the house and put my arm around his waist and helped him home.

But then confused feelings came over me. Seeing him again after so long reminded me about all the times we'd had together. I went to the kitchen, where Grandma found me sitting at the kitchen table. She must have sensed what I was thinking and tried to explain how I'd become a different person over the last few months and asked if I really wanted to go back to the life I had lived before.

I was upset and in two minds. On the Monday morning I went to school and hid in the laneway. When the school bell rang and I was all by myself, I kept looking for the horse and cart, hoping Dad would come and take me away. But he never came. I lost touch with him and the need to be with him gradually faded from my mind. I was now heading in a different direction and leaving my past life behind.

IN LOVE

*

In the last part of my final year at school, I was drawn to a girl call Pat, who was in the same grade as me. We became very friendly. Every day after school, we walked to the top of her street and talked for a few minutes before I went to my job at the box factory. It was all very sweet and innocent, a sort of puppy love between us. On Saturday afternoons, Pat went to the pictures with her girlfriend. I asked Grandma could I work for just half a day so I could go to the pictures and sit with Pat but got the same answer every time. "You're too young for that sort of stuff, you have to work to pay your way." I was determined nothing was going to stop me. I made up my mind to sit with Pat. I knew Grandma kept her spare money on top of the wardrobe in her bedroom. Because she'd denied me my freedom, I didn't feel a bit guilty about taking a ten-shilling note to make up my wages. After all, it was my hard- earned money. On Saturday mornings, I worked as fast as I could till it was time to go to the pictures and meet Pat. I was like my Dad when it came to flashing my money around; I tried to impress Pat with a bag of popcorn or a packet of Jaffas.

We were no different from the other kids at the matinee who rushed to sit in the front or the back seats when the doors opened. We rolled Jaffas down the aisle and stamped our feet while we waited for our cartoon, Pluto, then our serial, The Green Hornet. Did he survive the plunge over the cliff? At interval time if I had money, I would get the lolly boy's attention and buy two ice creams. The feature movie was usually a Tom Mix or a Laurel and Hardy. I didn't care. I was too taken up with resting my hand within a whisker of Pat's hand and had little thought of the movie. I was trying to pluck up enough courage to hold her hand. My primary school days were over and I began working full -time. I'd done reasonably well in my final year; except for my English and spelling, my marks were good enough to go to the Collingwood Technical School. I badly wanted to go there, but Uncle George put a stop to that and arranged a job for me. I was thirteen years of age when I was sent to work in my school shorts. The factory was called Peelshive Wooden Products. They made an assortment of wooden gadgets such as bath mats and long handle shovels for bakers' ovens. I know now Uncle George was using me as a tool in his hate for my father and his mother for allowing me to sleep under the same roof as him.

Pat and I had been going out for several months now and every day after work, I'd peddle my bike for all I was worth and meet her on the steps of the Fitzroy Town Hall for a few precious minutes. Her parents were strict like Grandma; every moment of our spare time we had to account for. Meanwhile, a strong desire was developing between us. I think we both wanted more than holding hands. Sitting on the steps and going to a matinee was not what we wanted. It was Pat who suggested we should go bike riding instead of wasting our Saturday afternoons and so the following Saturday we met and rode our bikes to Dights Falls. For the next two hours we sat on the cliff overlooking the river, watching the water flow over the falls and continue on its way before disappearing behind a tree lined bend.

For the past three Saturdays, it had been on my mind to tell Pat about my secret hiding place. I imagined the two of us being alone and in a world of our own. It was the thought of rejection that had stopped me. But this day I overcame my fears and told her about the black fellows' cave hidden in the bamboo sticks. This excited Pat and she jumped up from the ground, brushed the dry grass away from her dress and started to run towards the bamboo sticks. I followed her down the embankment and once again we held hands as we threaded our way to the cave. Pat was thrilled to share my secret and promised not to tell anyone. It was to be our secret meeting place forever.

For weeks we rode our bikes to the cave and each time we brought something to make ourselves more comfortable. We'd light a fire and sometimes roast potatoes. It was our kingdom. Around four o'clock we'd pack our things into a bag and leave them in the corner of the cave. Sure enough, the next Saturday they would still be there.

After nine months, I had not made much progress with my job. I was working a wooden lathe eight hours a day and turning out hundreds of wooden plugs for nine-gallon beer kegs. Grandma still insisted I bring home my twenty-eight shillings pay packet unopened, then she'd hand me back four shillings pocket money. To make a little extra money for myself, I still worked at the wood factory on Saturday mornings.

If it were not for my secret relationship with Pat, I would have left Grandma's place. I wanted my freedom. I felt I was deprived of everything; little money and no freedom, not like when I was with my Dad. It was all to change so suddenly. Pat and I were crouching around the fire, like we had done many times, waiting for our potatoes to roast and our knees were touching. I wanted to be closer to Pat. Only the thought of rejection stopped me. Pat must have read my thoughts. Suddenly she said, "Are you going to kiss me?" Those were the most beautiful words I had ever heard. That was all the encouragement I needed and it was the start of our intimate relationship. Our visits to the cave over the next five weeks became more intense. Our cave was like a home to us. Then it all came to an end. I still have very clear memories of the day we were sitting on the front steps of the Fitzroy Town Hall holding hands, when Pat broke the news to me that in five weeks' time her parents were moving permanently to New Zealand. I was devastated. The one person who understood me was, through no fault of her own, being taken away from me. I felt as if my whole world had caved in. For the first time in my life, I had found someone who cared for me and now I was never going to see her again. I did not realise it at the time, it was not losing Pat that caused the pain. I had a serious problem not being able to handle rejection. It was to live with me for the better part of my life.

Our visits to the cave over the next five weeks became more intense. We talked and talked about me saving enough money and following her to New Zealand. Finally, the time arrived when I was going to meet Pat and sit on the steps for a few precious last minutes before we said goodbye. For those minutes, we just cuddled and seemed to be lost for words. Then it was time to walk to the top of her street, which was a part of our life now. My heart was full of sadness as we embraced for the last time. Pat's eyes were full of tears and I knew if I dared to blink, a flood would cover my face. For a brief moment, Pat stood at the front gate, both our hands reaching out for each other. Then she disappeared beyond my flood of tears. Over the next weeks, I received two letters from

Pat. I did try to answer them, but each time, because of my lack of English and spelling, I lost confidence and tore up anything I attempted.

Today, the only remains of the cave are a small cavity in the side of the embankment where hundreds of names are scratched on the wall. There is also a pathway that the cave made way for Sunday walkers to take a leisurely stroll to the falls. When I take a walk along the pathway, I stop at the small cavity and think of my first love.

RESTLESS

*

I was now on my own and my world had fallen apart. I was becoming restless with the life I was leading, working five days a week and Grandma taking my full pay of twenty-eight shilling for my board, since I started my Saturday morning job. I wanted my freedom. I always had this feeling I didn't belong there, living with a sister and an uncle who found fault with whatever I did. When I told Grandma I intended to leave, she didn't try to talk me out of it.

On my last evening, Grandma was standing over the kitchen stove stirring a pot of Irish stew, while we sat around the table waiting for our tea. I was sitting there, jammed in my usual place in the far corner, where I always had to wait for the others to finish eating before I could leave the table. The kitchen was so small I often wondered how Grandma managed all those years to cook and look after nine people. Suddenly, I got a blast from Uncle George. He began raving on about how I would finish up on the streets, a drunk like my Dad. If it wasn't for Aunty Phyllis, who was trying to defend me, I think I might have stabbed him with the bread knife on the table. If ever I hated a man, it was my uncle at that moment. It was one of those rare times I wanted Dad to be there, to punch him up.

The next morning, I left. Grandma gave me a hug and said, "You're just like your Dad." I wondered what Grandma meant by that comment. Did she mean I would follow in Dad's footsteps and lead the same life? It's too late now to tell my Grandma how she pointed me in the right direction that turned my life around. I feel sure if she could see me now, a smile would broaden her face.

FREEDOM

*

I was sixteen and five months old when I walked out of the house with my few possessions packed in a medium-sized suitcase. I was now on my own. I had closed the door, which once had taken me in when I was in despair. The week I left Grandma's, I rented a room in King William St, Fitzroy, for ten shillings a week, changed my job and gave up my Saturday one. Now I had all the freedom I wanted. On the Monday morning I started work at a small furniture factory in Little Bourke Street. I was very contented working with the other tradesmen, six Chinese men. Every piece of furniture was handmade; crystal cabinets, wardrobes and dressing tables. I was really keen to learn the trade. I made sure I came to work early and lit the kerosene stove, so the three pots of glue crystals melted and were ready for the Chinese cabinet makers to start work. The only machine in the factory was a small cross-saw, with a drill for dowelling attached to the side of the machine.

In my first week I was allowed to use the machine and soon I was doing little dowelling jobs and liked what I was doing. My boss seldom came to the workroom, so he must have been satisfied with my work. I received a two and sixpence rise the first and the second week and to my surprise, I received a five shilling rise the following pay day. I had only been working for three weeks and had received three pay increases.

On the following Monday morning, it all went wrong. I don't know if I was over- confident while using the machine drilling pieces of wood. I had my back to the saw, which I had just switched on a minute earlier. There wasn't a guard to protect the saw blade. Standing with my back to the saw, I was talking to one of the Chinese workers. I became careless and, without looking, I went to pick up a piece of wood next to the running blade. Instead, I put my fingers on the top of the saw blade. I was lucky I didn't cut my four fingers off; they were pointing down towards the spinning blade and this saved them. I was taken to hospital to have my fingers stitched, and on the following Friday, when I went to receive my pay, I was sacked.

LUNCH BOY

*

Despite this setback, there were plenty of jobs advertised in The Age. I soon got a simple job in a shoe factory. For the first couple of hours, I felt confident in what I was doing. I worked well with the other men. I thought I wouldn't mind learning the shoe trade. There was nothing I couldn't do here in time. It looked pretty easy to me. Suddenly, I felt a tap on my shoulder. I looked around and saw the factory foreman smiling at me. "How would you like to be lunch boy Jumbo?" For a moment, I was taken aback. I could feel myself tightening up. My lack of education flashed through my mind. How the hell am I going to write the orders down? But I had no choice. I didn't want to risk losing my job. Taking the pad and pencil from the foreman, I faintly heard him say, "Start from the top end of the factory and make sure you don't miss anybody."

Walking slowly towards the man who was cutting shoe patterns I thought, "He looks too old to want any lunch." When the pattern cutter yelled out, "I want a pie and a vanilla slice, boy," I became flustered. I had no idea how to spell vanilla slice. By the time I had gone around the factory, my writing pad was a mess. I didn't know who had ordered what. I started to panic. I went to the men's toilet and locked myself in. For a while I felt safe there with my notepad. At first, I tried to rewrite the orders and hoped I could remember the rest. At the lunch shop, my confidence started to come back when the fat lady behind the counter gave me a warm smile. I handed her the note pad. She had a quick look and said softly to me, "I think you had better tell your boss you lost the lunch order and bring me another one."

Looking straight into her eyes, I felt my face turning red. I was sinking into the ground. Not another word was spoken. Our locked eyes said everything. I don't remember walking out of the shop. I just kept thinking about what the lady had said. Slowly I made my way back to the factory, thinking to myself, "How can I go through with this, me trying to write down all the lunch orders? No, I can't do it. I won't go back. I'll go to my hiding place by the river. I'll be safe there; no one can find me in the bamboo sticks." My lack of education hadn't worried me until then. I can still remember the bad feelings I had that day. At an early age, I was carrying a personal grudge against society. I was never given a chance in life. When I was a kid, I was kicked from pillar to post, had very little education, no home life and put to work early. I was feeling a lot better by the time I reached the river. The water looked good and it wasn't long before my feet were dangling in it. As I sat on the bank watching the water wind its way between the rocks, leaving little waterfalls in its path, my mind started to wander into another world. Suddenly I was a cabin boy on a whaling ship. A fierce storm was blowing the ship towards a reef. The captain panicked; he gave orders to abandon ship. I grabbed the helm from the captain and steered the ship safely away from the reef. I was a hero.

I jumped up from the river bank and suddenly remembered the lunch money in my pocket. Slowly, I retreated into the bamboo sticks. Now I felt really safe. Crouching close to the ground, I stacked the money into neat little piles. After counting it several times, I realised I had one pound and twelve shillings. "It's a fortune. What am I going to do with this money? It's not my fault I can't read or write properly," I kept repeating to myself. "I will keep the money. It's my mother's family's fault, not mine. If I had been given the chance, I could have been the best at school. All my Uncle George wanted was for me to go out to work and pay my way"

Next morning, I walked down to the paper shop to buy The Age to see what jobs were going. I noticed there were lots of jobs for lunch boys. "Why not? They put me here. I don't owe anything to anyone. I will look after myself first."

I decided to take a job in a furniture factory. This time, I gave a false name and address. It was safer that way. I pretended to write down everything and when I'd collected all the orders and the money, I would head straight for my hiding den. By the end of the first week, I'd had five different jobs and when I counted the money, it came to almost nine pounds. "It's a lot better than working for two pounds a week," I thought I was pretty smart, making all that money. Over the weekend, I worked out a plan to apply for jobs at the bigger factories. The more people, the more money.

On the Monday, I got a job at a woolen mill. Well, this was the jackpot. I had to finish all the orders by nine o'clock, morning teas and lunches. I would say I will bring back the change, all the time it was building up my bank. By the third week, I had lost all thought of having a conscience about my new enterprise. I was making money and I found I was becoming popular just like my Dad was with his mates. I was easy with money as I knew tomorrow, I could get more than I needed. Whenever I began to worry about what I was doing, I thought of my childhood as an excuse. Things were going along fine. I didn't have to get a job as often now as I was making a lot of money from the big factories. It's so easy, I thought. I knew what would happen if I got caught. I might go to jail or be put in a boys' home, but I still could not resist the easy life I was leading. The temptation was still too great. There were times when I thought of saving my money and going to New Zealand to find Pat but being with my mates seemed to put all such thoughts out of my mind. For a while I became the most travelled lunch boy in the business, with no thought of getting a permanent job.

The end came on a Friday morning. On the previous day, I'd really cleaned up at an iron foundry and had decided to take the day off and spend some of my new found wealth with my mates. I was walking down Smith Street, looking in shop windows, when a hand touched my shoulder and spun me around. It was the pattern cutter from the shoe factory. In a loud voice, he said, "I'll have a pie and a vanilla slice, boy. On the house." After the fright and running for dear life from the pattern cutter, all thoughts of continuing to be a lunch boy disappeared from my mind. More than once in the past, I'd looked over my shoulder, wondering if a face I'd just passed in the crowd recognised me. So, meeting the pattern cutter was a blessing in disguise for me.

ANOTHER JOB

*

My next job was working in a shoe repair shop in Collingwood. It was buried among never-ending rows of brick factories. When work finished, people from Foy and Gibson factories walked past our little shop six abreast, making their way home. It was also opposite the rat house where Dad and I once lived for a short time. I could see it from our workshop window and wondered if the rats were still running freely at night. The thought of that attack still lingered deeply in my mind. For the next couple of months, I considered becoming a cobbler, but the thought of collecting such a small wage each week kept nagging away at me.

Most afternoons my boss left me in charge of the shop. I seemed to spend a lot of time in the shop on my own. I had this job to do every Thursday that took up most of the day, riding my bike with a big wire basket tied to the handlebars, loaded with brown paper parcels. I was told to be very careful and talk to no one. I must have delivered a parcel to every hotel and factory in Fitzroy. One Thursday morning, my curiosity got the better of me and I opened a parcel. To my surprise, I realised I was being used as a decoy to deliver four- placed racing cards. My boss was a bookmaker. He ran the shoe shop as a cover up and that's why he spent a lot of time in the spare room; I guess he was taking bets on the horses whenever the phone rang.

BACK ON THE BOTTLE CART

*

*Working and surviving on a small wag*e and being used this way, did not appeal to me. Barney Ball didn't hesitate when I told him I wanted to hire a horse and cart and go bottleoing on my own, as Dad and I were no longer living together. Barney asked me what my Dad was doing; he'd not seen him for several weeks. I had seen him and told Barney he was selling his bottles at a yard in Fitzroy. I sensed Barney wasn't happy when he heard this. He said, "When you see your old man again, tell him to come and see me about the five pounds he borrowed."

As I drove the horse away from the bottle yard, I thought of my Dad letting Barney down. It worried me and after I'd finished my day's work, I walked up to the Napier Hotel where I found him. He wasn't too bad, as the afternoon was still early. He seemed surprised when he looked up and saw me standing there. "There's my boy," he said.

To hear those words once meant so much to me. Now it only gave me a feeling of sadness. I asked Dad about owing Barney five pounds. He denied it, then promptly asked me for a loan. I gave him ten shillings and walked out of the hotel with a feeling that I would never be like him. But all the things he'd taught me I was going to use to my advantage. The first couple of days dealing with people weren't as easy as I first thought. After paying Barney for the hire of the horse and cart, I was only making a few shillings for a day's work. Without Dad to back me up, I knew I was paying more for my bottles and scrap than my Dad did.

The next morning, I decided to work the back lanes of Clifton Hill and yodel "bottleo." As I drove the horse along the long, narrow cobbled lanes at a walking pace, I stood on the cart, stretching to see over the top of the corrugated iron fences, searching for burnt-out bath heaters or stacks of empty beer bottles against a fence, anything of value.

When I came across a good call, I'd sing out "Bottleo" and kick the fence with my foot to make myself heard, until someone came out to see what all the noise was about. With my confidence back, I would say with my best smile, "Do you want to sell your bottles, lady?" I always gave money, like a shilling, for a bag or two of bottles or a bath heater. As my Dad said, "If you put something in their hand, it's not stealing, that's a deal." Quite often I had an unhappy customer, but as the days passed, I got more and more determined to be like my Dad when I made a deal.

OLD FRIENDS

*

When I was younger, there was a boy who used to hang around the bottle yard and sometimes I went to his place instead of going to the hotel with Dad. Because we moved from place to place, I lost touch with Tommy. I got a surprise one day to see Tommy working with the other men, washing bottles and stacking them on drying racks. As I walked between the wash tubs, he said, "Don't you remember me, Jumbo? It's Tommy."

He had changed a lot since I saw him last. He had grown tall and was full of confidence as he joked with the other men. I waited around the yard until he finished work and we soon became good friends. I spent a lot of my time at his place and it sort of became my second home. Many a night I had a meal and slept there. Betty, Tommy's mother, liked me being round Tommy because she knew I didn't drink beer; Tommy was starting to drink beer, just like his father. It was Tommy's idea I should learn some of the old-time dances and when I thought I was good enough, we ventured to the Saturday night dance.

At that stage of my life, I was still very shy of girls, even though I had experienced what I thought it was like to be in love. It took me most of the night to pluck up enough courage to ask a girl for a dance, let alone to ask one if she'd like a soft drink at interval. I couldn't handle it if I was refused. Tommy was the complete opposite. His confidence on the dance floor had no equal and when it came to jitter- bugging, he left all the other dancers in awe. Many a night I stood at the hall door, watching Tommy take home a heart he had won for the night.

There were also good times after a night of dancing. If it was a moonlit night, we'd pack a few things together and ride our bikes to Clarke field, with our rifles slung across our backs. We'd arrive in the early hours of the morning and wait for daybreak before we started shooting rabbits. One Sunday morning, I came across a little gully. I had never seen so many rabbits in one place and it became a regular spot. We'd lay on our stomachs and fire away 'til most of our bullets were used, then gather up the rabbits and at lunch time make the long ride back to Melbourne.

We always seemed to strike a headwind both ways. It was hard going with the rifles and a bike load of rabbits. When we arrived home, we'd be completely exhausted and say, "Never again." But we'd soon forget about our aches and pains and when the time was right, we would wait for a full moon and ride our bikes again. Tommy wanted me to work with him washing bottles. I said, no, I could earn more money on the bottle cart.

I got an idea when I was at a furniture factory watching men working away at their wood machines. All the small wooden offcuts were stacked in a large pile next to the brick furnace, waiting to be burnt with the sawdust and shavings. I asked the manager of the factory if I could have the wood. He was only too happy to get rid of it. Each day after I finished my day's work, I drove my horse and cart to the factory and before long, I had loaded several bags of firewood.

I had no trouble in selling the wood as it was ideal for burning in chip heaters, or I'd exchange the wood for bottles. I was soon making good money. There were days when I'd see Dad on the road and we'd pull our carts up side by side and talk for a few minutes. He would always say, "How are you going, Jumbo?" and ask how was I holding, after all he was my dad. One Friday afternoon, I asked Dad what had happened at the camp when I suddenly left to go to Grandma's. "I sold whatever we had to the rabbit buyer and moved after you left." I also wanted to know why he hadn't come to see me. He said sometimes he'd drive past the school and see me playing in the playground, then drive away. "It was better for you to stay where you were than for me to get mixed up in your life again." Those few words were like gold to me.

Tommy and I started to hang around the billiard room in Johnson Street next to the Austral Theatre. It was a long and dingy room, with several billiard tables taking up most of the space. A row of wooden seats ran along each side of the wall on a raised platform. The pool table at the far end of the room was reserved for the best players. Men would vie for a seat to watch, or have a side bet on the big game that took place most nights. The smoke from a dozen cigarettes drifted across the room and hung close to the table lights. Tommy and I were never allowed to venture past the third table because of our age. When these games were being played, we'd watch with envy, hoping one day we would be good enough to play on the big table.

There had been a time in the nineteen thirties and forties when it was the headquarters of a street gang called the 'Don Mob'. The Don Room was a hangout for all types, some of whom would eventually turn to crime, including murder and spend time in jail, or die early. I somehow managed to keep one step ahead of all this and never got into any trouble. I was contented to work the bottle cart.

I was nearly seventeen years of age and was enjoying my life, even though I was mixing in pretty tough company. After work I went to the gym in Johnson Street, Fitzroy and met my mates. For the next couple of hours, we trained hard, wanting to be better than the thirty or more other boys in the gym, with one thought in mind, to become a main event fighter at Festival Hall. After a solid workout, we wanted a shower but most nights with only two showers, it was almost impossible. We got dressed in a lather of sweat. Across the road, the Birmingham Hotel was our meeting place. We talked about who was who at the gym while we had a few drinks. It didn't matter how much my mates tried; I never gave in to their demands 'have a beer, Jumbo.' Instead a glass of sarsaparilla was my favourite drink. I had seen what drinking beer had done to my Dad. In time, my mates understood and accepted me for what I was. I always left the pub after a short time and tried to take Tommy with me. He was more than liking the taste of beer and as the weeks passed by, he was mixing more with the wrong company. On a Saturday afternoon, with a few of the boys from the gym, we went to watch Fitzroy play. I could not help noticing the empty beer bottles scattered amongst the litter. It just seemed like yesterday that I half-filled my sack bag with empty beer bottles. At 17 years of age, I was not as desperate to survive as I had been as a nine-year-old kid. I stopped going to the footie after a while. Tommy and his mates would pick a fight for no reason at all. It wasn't what I came to a football match for. I had seen too much street fighting with my Dad. I also moved out of Tommy's place because of his drinking. We had drifted apart and it was time to move on. Tommy went downhill fast after I left. He got the sack from Barney's bottle yard for missing too many days, then he served a short time in prison for stealing. The morning I left his mother said, "Tommy will finish up a drunk just like his father." Little did she realise how true those words were.

MY MOTHER

*

My mother was living in Collingwood. Jack, my brother who I hardly knew, had just returned from World War II and was living at my mother's place. I decided to go and live with Jack because at the time I wanted to get to know my brother better. I gave the bottle cart up and took a job in an electro-plating factory. My brother didn't have the time of day for me. It gave me the same feeling of not being wanted that had haunted me when I'd lived with my siblings before. After a short stay, I moved on. I guess I had inherited some of my Dad's ways. I moved to a rooming house in Fitzroy and once again changed my job. I started work for a furniture factory in Bell Street, Preston. I worked in the veneer room and at doing other little jobs. I really liked my job and before long I was offered an apprenticeship.

After work, I still went to the gym for a workout and sometimes to have my tea in the same Chinese café where my Dad and I had many a meal. I was happy in my new surroundings and soon made friends with the people who rented two of the other rooms. They had a daughter about my age named Joan and we soon struck up a friendship. We went dancing at the Exhibition Buildings on a Saturday night. It was only a ten-minute walk into the city and sometimes we had supper after the dance finished. We were very good friends and not once did we hold hands in the time I rented a room there. It was always the same problem I had. I couldn't face the thought of her rejecting me. I was still going to the gym. An ex-boxer of note, Billy Rainbow, who ran the gym, took more than a personal interest in me and said I had a future as a boxer if I was taken along in the amateur ranks for a couple of years. I have often wondered how far I could have gone if I'd stayed in Melbourne. I was training for my first amateur fight when fate took me in another direction.

GRANDMA

*

My Dad left a message at the bottle yard that Grandma wanted to see me. On the following Sunday, I went to see Grandma, dressed in my best clothes. I was happy when Donny opened the front door; I will never forget that man. Everybody else was out, to my relief. I think she was surprised when I told her I was working in a furniture factory and was going to have my first amateur fight soon. We talked for a long time about my Dad and how he had changed when he met my mother. I said I would never drink beer and I wouldn't be like my Dad. Then Grandma told me she saw me one Saturday morning collecting bottles and had decided she would do something about it because she was worried I was going to finish up like my father. She had written a letter to my oldest brother Bob, who I hardly remembered and was now living in a small country town in New South Wales, running a plaster factory. I partly read his letter offering me a job. Grandma seemed pleased when we talked about the letter.

When I lived at Grandma's for a short time, my brother Bob was away at the war. Grandma made me sit at the kitchen table and try to write a letter to him, something I could never do. For an hour or more I sat in front of my writing pad, then gave up. How could I write to someone I never knew? After a lot of pressure from Grandma, I said, "I will go and work for my brother."

A CHALLENGE

*

At the time, I was still living in Fitzroy and decided to walk down to Victoria Street, Richmond and buy some new clothes for my trip away. I saw a green suit with white squares in a shop window. I thought it was perfect to wear with my white and brown perforated shoes and my green tie with a hula girl painted on it. The trousers were three sizes too big for me around the waist, but the shopkeeper said it would be all right and gave me a belt to hold them up. "Don't worry, the coat will cover your trousers."

I parted with four pounds and thought I was just it when I walked out of the shop with the suit tucked under my arm. On the Saturday night I went to a dance with Joan and wore my green suit for the first time. I had a lot of trouble keeping my trousers up because of the overlap. Finally, Joan solved the problem with a large pin.

LEAVING MELBOURNE

*

It had been arranged by my Grandma I would meet my brother at the Fitzroy football ground on Sunday afternoon and travel back to NSW on a bus with him. When I arrived at the football ground, I saw a coach parked outside the clubrooms with NSW number plates and thought it was best if I waited near the coach until someone came out as I was too shy to go in to the club rooms.

After a while, two men wearing football blazers appeared. They walked over to where I was standing and wanted to know if I was waiting for someone. I said I was waiting for my brother. Then the bus started to fill up with a lot of men wearing the same blazers. I saw my brother walking towards me. We hardly said a word. I boarded the bus and made my way down the aisle towards the back and found a window seat. I was given plenty of strange looks and I heard someone say, "It's Bob's young brother." I felt every bump in the road. My brother sat in the centre of the bus with his friends as if I didn't exist. It never occurred to him to come and sit with me so we could get to know each other when I needed his assurance most. The men drank nonstop for the first couple of hours. I was offered a drink from a bottle of beer several times. A joke was made when I refused. Little did they know how much I disliked the stuff.

As the coach ate away the miles into the night, the continuing sound of the motor purring sent a feeling of sleepiness through each of us. Then there was silence for the first time, except for the necessary stop on the side of the road, when a voice in the darkness outside the coach made a crude remark about someone's prick. Then there was laughter when another dirty remark was made. Once again, there was silence and I soon fell into a deep sleep for the last part of the journey. I was awakened by a voice, "We should be home in a few minutes." Slowly, the slumbering bodies in their seats began to stir and come to life. Another voice was heard above the chatter. "Has anybody got the time?" The fellow sitting next to me, who had been using my shoulder as a pillow, answered his call. I was wide awake now and was anxious to know where I was.

I pressed my face against the bus window as we crossed the bridge and felt the rubber rolling over the wooden sleepers. The reflection from the full moon lit up the river. Weeping Willows hung lazily over the river banks, undisturbed by the flowing water, as we crossed the Murray into NSW. That was my first glimpse of the river. For the next minute or two we continued along the uneven surface and when a street light appeared a voice said, "We're home boys." As the bus entered the main street, the bus driver changed down another gear and a lone car parked outside a hotel was the only thing I saw to remind me that people might live there. What sort of a place was this? The stillness of the night made me feel a little unsure. My thoughts were back in Melbourne with my mates. I convinced myself I had made a bad mistake and in the morning, I would go back to my friends as soon as I could. Suddenly, the bus took a sharp turn and stopped outside a hotel. Men scrambled for their bags and made a rush for the door as if there wasn't a minute to lose and disappeared towards the waiting car lights. My sleeping partner was in no hurry to follow his mates. He handed me my suitcase from the overhead rack without saying a word. When it was all clear, I made my way to the coach door. The driver had already started the motor and was in a hurry to leave after such a long drive. I was all alone except for the small light above the hotel door, where moths and insects kept flirting with death. I stood watching them and wondered if I was any better off, as I waited for my brother, who had joined some of the other men and gone into the hotel. I was getting agitated at being left alone. "Where is the bastard? What in the hell am I doing here, standing outside a hotel late at night? For what, I don't know?"

I was now thinking about my Dad and the times I spent outside hotels waiting for him and here I was doing it again for someone I didn't care about. My brother finally appeared at the hotel door and beckoned me to follow him to a room. I was told not to unpack my things, as tomorrow I would be moving to a boarding house. Then he left the room. That's all the conversation we had. At last, I was on my own and soon fell asleep. My brother woke me the next morning. For a moment I didn't know where I was. I was confused, seeing my brother standing by the bedside. Then all my thoughts came back to me. "Why am I sleeping in a strange bed?" I was shown where the shower was and the dining room. This was all new to me. I had never slept in a hotel room before or eaten in a plush room like the one I was standing in now. My brother was sitting at a table eating his breakfast with another man. For some reason, I wasn't asked to join them, so I had breakfast on my own. My brother asked me if I had any better clothes than the ones I'd worn on the bus. I said I had a grey suit but that it was the fashion in Melbourne to wear loud clothes. He wasn't a bit impressed with my answer.

A NEW LIFE

*

My brother didn't waste any time with me; there was no showing me the sights of my new home. We went straight to the plaster works where I was working within the hour of waking up. After my first day at work, I was taken to a boarding house. At the rear of the yard was a large tin shed which someone had the bright idea of dividing into ten bedrooms. My room was so small there was only space for a bed and a small wardrobe. The room I'd left in Melbourne was far better; at least I could walk around without touching the bed. This sort of accommodation was still to be a part of my life for a few more years. To me, it was just another place to sleep, except this time I had real company.

I was to share my life with nine other roommates who were so different to the boys I knew in Melbourne. Drinking and smoking hardly existed in their minds. We had all come from different country towns from all over Victoria and New South Wales, seeking permanent work. Our bathroom and toilets were well away from our rooms. It was just as if you were in a caravan park walking to the showers. I felt a little shy when I entered the dining room for my first evening meal. I stood for a moment at the door and was surprised to see several young women having their dinner with some of my roommates I'd met earlier in the evening. Two young men caught my eye and beckoned me to their table. One of the boys had arrived the day before to start a new job with the railways. His name was Dick Turbine. I felt at ease straight away with Dick and we were to become good friends until our destinations in life took us in different directions. Before long, I was beginning to learn there was another life to the one I had led for the previous seventeen years. There was very little drink and no fighting. Going back to my old ways was a thing of the past. My new life was now serving me in another way. I didn't have to mix with drink or be pestered with smoking or go to the gym to prove myself. There was only one man and a boy working in my brother's plaster factory. I was a good worker and a quick learner. It wasn't long before I was making plaster sheets and within a few months I was running the factory. My brother was a compulsive gambler and he spent more time on the race course than working in the factory. I was very happy with my new life and friends. All my mates at the gym had given me three weeks before I was back in Fitzroy. How wrong they all were. It was the beginning of another chapter in my life.

LIVING IN A COUNTRY TOWN

*

Living in a country town exposed you to different sports. Football on a Saturday afternoon had meant only one thing to me, to make money for my Dad by collecting empty beer bottles. Except for kicking a paper football or one wrapped in a sock, it never occurred to me I might be good at the game. I was not a bit interested in playing when two boys at the boarding house said they played in a minor league and their club was looking for new players. I decided to have a training run. To my surprise, I found I was very quick and determined. I played the whole season as first rover and came third in the club's Best and Fairest. The following year, I was recruited to the Ovens and Murray League, which I played for three years before I retired for personal reasons. When I tried something new, I had to prove to myself I wasn't a failure. My early life as a child was still deeply imbedded in my mind.

CHURCH FELLOWSHIP

*

I was content to be with my mate. In lots of ways, he was like me. Dick avoided people more than I did. I decided to go to church with Dick one Sunday night for the first time and for the next few weeks I never missed going to church with my new friend. One Sunday night after church, the Minister invited us back to fellowship. Dick refused, and I didn't want to go by myself, so we went back to our rooms.

The following week, the Minister asked us again. Dick didn't want to go. He was a sort of a loner; he liked to spend his time in his room making aeroplanes out of balsa wood. I decided to go by myself. I liked these evenings. It was another world to what I had known in the past. The more I mixed with these young people, the more I wanted to be a part of their life. Our church made arrangements for our fellowship to visit another church for a social evening.

There was a girl I had a crush on, so I was hoping we would ride in the same car. My luck was out. The girls were chauffeured by a lady driver. The boys went in a separate car with the Minister. Our social evening was full of harmless fun. We played several different games. In one game, we had to write down answers to a simple quiz. I was given a pencil and a piece of paper and paired off with a partner. I became flustered and embarrassed at the thought of not being able to spell what I had to write down. I had to escape from my partner. I made the excuse I wasn't feeling too well. Later on, we played a game called passing the life saver. We were put in three different groups in a straight line, with a match between our lips, the girl at the head of the line had the life saver on a match held between her lips then passed the life saver to the next boy without dropping it. I waited for my turn to take the life saver from Liz, the girl I liked. I was excited at the thought of brushing her lips. I don't remember dropping the life saver. There was laughter. I went all red and could not stop blushing.

Later that evening, I managed to get up the courage to ask Liz if she would like to go to the pictures. Liz was a local girl; her family owned a large wheat station several kilometers from town. Over the past weeks I had been enjoying my football, especially when Liz was watching. For the following few weeks Liz was my greatest fan until, suddenly, I was dumped. Once again, I felt my fear of rejection had worked against me. Liz said I was too shy for her. "Why can't you be more aggressive, like the way you play football?" After this experience, I felt I wasn't ready for a permanent relationship. Spending times with my mates was more important to me at this time of my life than chasing girls.

HARVEST TIME

*

It was getting close to Christmas and I was thinking about going back to Melbourne for a holiday. Two years had passed since I had made a decision that changed my life for the better. My two mates, Victor Lovett and Ken Rushgrove, were now making a name for themselves in boxing circles. I had been following their careers in the Sporting Globe with more than a passing interest. They were both fighting main events at the old West Melbourne Stadium. I would think to myself, "If I'd stayed in Melbourne and taken Billy Rainbow's advice, my life would be so different to what I am doing now." The plaster works was having its problems. There was a building recession and my brother was too lazy to look for new orders. He was relying on his gambling to survive.

Frank, who lived next door to the plaster works, was looking for a young man to help his brother harvest the wheat crop. I thought if I worked until the harvest was finished, I could save enough money for a decent holiday. Oliver was in his late fifties, slightly bald, with an oversized stomach. I knew very little about him except he came into town once a week for his supplies, then visited his brother. To me, he was just a harmless old man. I was happy to take the job, even though I had never driven a tractor or a car before. I packed a few clothes to be ready for an early start the next morning.

Oliver was waiting at the farm gate with his two dogs and was relieved when he saw me pedalling in the distance. He said he had been let down many times before by workers. I put my bike in the back of his ute and waited for him to drive through the farm gate so I could close it and fasten the chain around the fence post. It was still early morning, but the sun was already warning us it was going to be a scorcher of a day as we drove up a dirt track towards the house. The heads of wheat were ripe and rusty looking. Oliver said they were ready to be harvested. We would have to work nonstop to finish the harvest in case of rain. I said I was willing to work as I wanted the money for a holiday.

As the ute approached the top of a slight rise, in the distance were several large sheds. I strained my eyes to see the house. It was nowhere to be seen. I thought it must have been on another part of the property. Oliver stopped the ute between the two sheds. It was then I realised there was no house, just a couple of old rusty tin sheds. Close by there was a vegetable garden and a clothesline with a pair of pants hanging by one leg. A German shepherd lay beside his kennel with his head resting on his two front paws, quite undisturbed by the sound of the bike being unloaded from the back of the ute. He lazily lifted his head for a moment as I wheeled the bike past him. Walking ahead of me, Oliver made a remark, "He is my old favourite, not long for this world." Oliver pushed the door open and said, "Come in and have some breakfast." The rusty iron shed with the dirt floor was his home, for how long I don't know. His ruffled bed was in one corner, with a wooden wardrobe next to it. One of the doors was just hanging by a thread. It looked as if the door was going to fall any moment. There were a few pieces of furniture scattered around. It was not what I expected; besides his new utility, Oliver drove a flash car and I thought he lived in a big house.

After I had eaten my breakfast, I was ready to work. Oliver picked up my bag with my few clothes and put them on his bed. I had already noticed there was only his bed and the thought had crossed my mind, "Where am I going to sleep?" We left the old rusty shed and walked towards one of the largest sheds I've ever seen. It was full of all types of modern machinery. I thought this shed was far superior to the one he was living in. First Oliver showed me how to drive the big tractor. After a few practice runs and turns, I soon got the hang of driving it. As the morning progressed, I was feeling the heat of the sun. I had little protection; my cricket cap was useless.

The sound of Oliver's words, "Finish this row and have lunch," was sweet music to my ears. I was more than ready for a break as I drove the tractor back to the shed for a well-earned rest. Oliver was concerned I was getting sunburnt and insisted I take my shirt off so he could rub sun cream on my back and neck. I had to tell him to stop rubbing my chest; it was the back of my neck that was burning.

I was enjoying my new work. My confidence was getting better with each run and I was starting to get the knack of stacking the wheat bags. Oliver was pleased with my effort when we finished at sunset. I was covered in red dust and once again, the sight of the tin shed was most welcome as I drove the tractor through the last gate. Our work was not finished yet. I had to fill the tractor with fuel and check the oil, while Oliver greased the tractor and harvester ready for the next day's work. I was totally exhausted as I entered the shed. All I wanted to do was lay down to regain some of my strength. Oliver took two bottles of beer from the gas refrigerator and put them on the kitchen table. Then he beckoned me to draw up a chair and join him. I refused the beer even though my throat was reaching out for something more than water. Thoughts of my father flashed through my mind. I refused and settled for a billy of tank water. The temptation after a day in the blazing sun still wasn't enough to sway me to have my first drink of beer. In the centre of the room was a tin bath supported by four rusty cast iron claw legs and a chip heater resting on a wooden makeshift stand, just like the one we used in Melbourne when I was a kid. Oliver started talking about how lonely he was living on his own all these years and when he died, there was no one to leave the farm to. I felt really sorry for him and said there must be ladies who wanted a husband. I didn't give much thought to what Oliver had said. I knew what it was like to be alone.

I lit the chip heater and soon a flow of warm water started to fill the bath. Oliver suggested I should have first bath. I did not hesitate. It looked inviting as I took my clothes off and stepped in. I felt relief with the feel of warm water over my body. For a few moments I was laying there in a world of my own, not realising Oliver was standing beside the bath with a cake of soap in his hand wanting to wash my back. I took it as a joke, and just laughed and said no thanks. For the next few minutes, I was enjoying the feel of the water. I had forgotten all about Oliver. I was thinking about the money I'd save for my holiday and what it would be like to see all my mates again, when I noticed Oliver walking towards the bath naked. I thought he wanted to have his bath and I attempted to get out when he stepped into the bath and fell on top of me. His hard penis was pressing into my stomach, and he mumbled something about I could have whatever I wanted if we played games.

My childhood memories came back to me, the thought of a swaggie trying to take advantage of me when my Dad was at the pub and other similar thoughts, raised my temper. I struggled for a moment and then gave him my best and left him lying on the floor. I got dressed quickly and rode my bike back to town. All my good plans had gone up in the air. I was two weeks behind with my board and no money. I was now without a job. My brother had closed down the plaster works and gone to Melbourne with his girlfriend.

I was ready to pack my few belongings and hitch hike back to Melbourne and work the bottle cart, when I met Oliver in the main street. He was looking for me and was very sorry for what he did. "It was the drink and please come back and finish the harvest. There would be no more trouble." He was very concerned, in case I had told anyone about the previous night. I said, "No." He then gave me ten pounds. The money was a blessing to me. I took it without feeling guilty. I felt I earned it. I went back to my boarding house and paid my board. The next morning, I arrived at the farm early for work. The first thing I noticed was a new single bed. We worked long hours harvesting the wheat. I was now handling the tractor as if I had been driving it all my life. Oliver was no problem; we were getting on well together.

After finishing our day's work, I had my bath, then Oliver had his bath. Oliver even suggested leaving the shed while I had my bath. I said there was no need for that. If he had other ideas, he never showed them again. After dinner, we played a game of cards and retired early. For the next two weeks, we worked fourteen hours a day and were more than halfway through the harvest. It was a hotter summer than usual; this was one of the reasons the harvest was early. Normally Oliver worked right through and finished the harvest in case there was rain. This time, he decided to finish early on Christmas Eve and start again on Boxing Day. I was pleased for the break and drove back to town with him.

CHRISTMAS DAY

*

My friend Dick was pleased to see me, as everyone from the boarding house had gone home for Christmas. Dick was having Christmas dinner with the owners of the boarding house, George and his wife and their son Robert. While having Christmas dinner, I think Dick had the same thoughts as I did, "What would it be like to share Christmas day with your own family?"

FINISHING THE HARVEST

*

Oliver had decided to stay Christmas night at his brother's place, so I would not have to ride the bike in the morning. We had now become firm friends. In one way, I was glad to see the last of the harvest. Oliver said it was a bumper crop and he would like me to work for him again. I received a nice pay. There was still no sign of my brother, or any orders for the plaster works, so I decided to catch a train to Melbourne and have a holiday.

OLD MEMORIES

*

I was now looking forward to catching up with my Dad and my two mates. I arrived at Spencer Street Station and decided to see if Joan and her family were still living at the boarding house where I'd had a room. I was greeted by her father, who was pleased to see me and wanted to know all about my new life. Then suddenly Joan appeared, carrying a baby in her arms. I got up from my chair and in my shy way said, "Hello Joan." It was her father who said, "Joan has a little baby boy." I could not hide the surprised look on my face. I don't know if I was embarrassed at that moment, or disappointed seeing her standing there holding a baby in her arms. I just felt I wanted to escape from the room. Was it because we had spent so much time together and I had never once attempted to hold her hand, let alone kiss her? I felt there was no reason to stay any longer. Feeling a little down, I decided to walk to Smith Street and have a Chinese meal. Memories of Gordon House lingered in my mind as I ate my meal. I then decided to catch a tram into the city and sleep in the same room I had shared as a child with my Dad. It was not to be. The room I wanted in Gordon House was already taken. The next morning, I had breakfast in Little Bourke Street, then decided to find my Dad.

It was about three o'clock when I finally found my Dad at the Sierra Sands Hotel in Fitzroy, with a couple of drinking mates who I had never seen him with before. The first thing he said was, "Hello Jumbo. Have you got a pound to spare?" We had very little to talk about. It was like two strangers meeting for the first time. I made an excuse and said I wanted to go to the gym and see my two old school mates.

SCHOOL MATES

*

It was about five o'clock when I walked through the gym door. The smell of sweat brought back old memories. The place was full of young men going through their daily routine. How times had changed in just a short time. I hardly recognised a soul. I was a total stranger as I walked amongst the 'would-be's'. I saw Ken working out on the punching bag. He looked up and said, "Hello Wattsie," and kept punching the bag. I waited until he finished his workout. Ken said, "How would you like to get into the ring with me now? I've got sixty fights under my belt?" I guess Ken never forgot the first time we met. I then went over and spoke to Victor. I felt like a stranger trying to be friendly. I walked out of the gym, this time forever.

DISAPPOINTING FAMILY

*

I was not enjoying my holiday. Grandma was on my mind. I decided to go and see her. Uncle George answered the door and coldly greeted me. Ma was away on a bus trip. I was not invited into the house. Once again, I journeyed back to Little Bourke Street and stayed the night at Gordon House and had breakfast at the same little café. For the rest of the day, I wandered wherever my thoughts took me. I decided to go and see my Dad once more. Maybe yesterday I was too hasty in my thinking. Today I might find him sober if I went a little earlier.

I stood at the front door of the same hotel and poked my head through the bar door. Watching my Dad, memories came flashing back. How many hours and days had I spent sitting on a bar stool waiting to take him home? There he was holding court, just like when I was a boy. I walked away with saddened thoughts. Tomorrow morning, I will catch a train back to where I have a real life. My intended holiday lasted less than a week.

BACK TO WORK

*

My brother and his friend Bill, who he met during the Second World War, served in the same division. When the war was over, my brother settled in a country town with Bill. He owned a monumental masonry business and he wanted me to work for him until the plaster factory found more work. To me it was just another job and at least I would be employed. It was the break of day when I walked into the work yard. Bill had already loaded up the Cheviot with tools and cement. The old nineteen thirty -six Chevy, with a dicky seat full of tools, was well and truly loaded down to the axles. The morning sun was already telling us it was going to be a scorcher. For the next hour, we drove in silence. Bill wasn't much of a talker; he was content to suck on his pipe as he sat behind the wheel of the Chevy. After another twenty minutes of driving, we turned off the main highway and made our way along a dirt road. I sighted the top of a headstone peeping above the tall, dry grass. In the background was a dilapidated shelter shed with part of its roof missing. The years of neglect had taken their toll. The iron front gate had come to grief long ago. It was partly buried by overgrown grass. At least I did not have to get out of the car to open the gate. We turned left into the cemetery and stopped for a moment as Bill took out the cemetery map to check the location of the gravesite. I walked over to the water tank to see if there was enough water for mixing concrete. At the same time, I was hoping the gravesite was close to where the gravel was dumped. Bill wandered off with the map in his hand to a freshly made track.

There had just recently been a funeral; the flowers were no more than a few days old. Just a little further on Bill was standing next to a gravesite. The dried flowers had long lost their meaning as they lay scattered over the grave. All life had left them long ago. "This is the one, George," yelled Bill. I had already checked the water tank and when I told him there wasn't much water, Bill went and had a look and decided to take the risk and do the job. The gravel and water were at least eighty yards from the grave. It was not the first time I'd mixed concrete with Bill. Over the previous two years, when the plaster works were slack, I'd helped him many times. My first job was to clear away the dry grass to make a place to mix the concrete, while Bill formed the boxing. For the next two hours, we mixed several batches of concrete before the double grave was finished. We hadn't stopped all morning. I was glad for the break as I sat in the shade under a large old gum tree for a well-deserved rest while Bill finished the last of the troweling. It was twelve o'clock and I was feeling hungry. With one thought, the sandwiches on the seat of the car. They felt warm from the morning sun and without thinking, I took a sandwich and started to eat it. Bill had not started to eat his sandwich. He first opened it to see if it was alright to eat and that's when I saw maggots dropping to the ground. I ran to the closest bush and vomited so much my stomach was sore for days. I worked with Bill for the next few weeks and every lunchtime, I could not face a sandwich. The plaster works started to get busy again. Bill wanted me to work with him full time, but I decided to go back and work in the factory.

NEW SCHOOL TEACHER

*

We were all having dinner in the dining room when the owner of the boarding house said, "You boys better behave yourselves tomorrow night. We have the new school teacher staying with us." This caused a bit of a laugh and a joke or two was made between us that she must be a bag.

The next night, we all arrived at the table early to wait for the new teacher from Melbourne to come down for dinner. That night has never faded from my mind. The five of us boys were sitting at the table. There was one vacant chair left for the school teacher. We decided to have a little fun to see who would ask her to our table. I was hoping it wouldn't be me and was relieved when it was Patrick who drew the shortest match. Then this attractive young woman appeared. For a moment she surveyed the room, not too sure of her next movement. Patrick caught her attention and pointed to the vacant chair next to him. She gave us all a lovely smile and walked towards us. We stood up and Patrick introduced us to Ruth. Her fresh presence made the meal most enjoyable. I hardly said a word at the table. The boys were trying their best to impress her. I was very shy. Occasionally, I'd glance in her direction when I thought she was busy talking to one of the other boys. Patrick asked her if she would like to come shooting rabbits with the boys tomorrow night after dinner. It was decided to have an early dinner and leave about five thirty in Patrick's A -model Ford. We had now finished dinner and I was about to leave the table when Ruth asked me what I did. I felt comfortable talking to her and after a while, my shyness partly left me. It was eleven thirty when the owner of the boarding house came in and said it was time the lights were turned off. I went back to my room and got a ribbing from my mates. They all said she liked me and Patrick didn't stand a chance. After talking to Ruth for so long, I made my mind up, I wanted to see more of her. Ruth had everything I didn't and I wanted to be part of it. She was well-educated and she was a lady and not the sort of woman my Dad lived with.

SHOOTING A RABBIT

*

We were all standing outside the front of the boarding house when Patrick arrived. We still had about three hours of daylight left when we piled into his A-model Ford. It was great fun, and we were full of laughter. A strange thing happened when we arrived at the end of the dirt track. Everyone jumped out of the car with their rifles, including me. We all thought Patrick was going to look after Ruth, as it was his date. I was about fifty yards down the track when I looked back. There was Ruth, standing all alone next to the car. Patrick had walked off without giving Ruth a thought. I looked around for Patrick, but he was nowhere to be seen. I waved to Ruth to come with me and said I was sorry she had been left behind; we thought Patrick was looking after you.

It was Ruth's first experience at shooting rabbits. She was enjoying the walk, but I had to tell her many times to be quiet, as she was frightening the rabbits before I had the chance to shoot. My childhood stood me in good stead. I knew how to stalk rabbits and how to locate the most likely place to find them. These rabbits had been hunted often. At the slightest sound of a twig being disturbed, they'd quickly disappear before one had a chance to raise the rifle. We had to be very quiet, and soon Ruth got the idea and I was able to take a shot. I stalked a rabbit that was too busy cleaning himself to notice me. I was only twenty yards away from it with Ruth close behind me. I shot it in the head and felt very proud. Ruth was a little upset when she saw the rabbit give its last couple of kicks before life left it. At first she protested, but I insisted she should try one shot. After showing Ruth what to do, she gave in and to my s urprise, she shot the rabbit in the back. The rabbit tried to drag itself into the bracken by its two front legs. I ran towards the rabbit and put it out of its misery. I asked Ruth to pick it up, but she refused. I said, "If you don't pick it up, what was the point of shooting it?" Ruth then picked up the rabbit by her thumb and one finger and handed it to me.

REJECTION

*

The driving force I possessed not wanting to be rejected, started when I was a child. Whatever the challenge was, I succeeded in getting my own way. I feel some of my problems came from working on the bottle cart, making sure I was doing deals to please my Dad. For several weeks, I was determined Ruth was going to be mine and nobody else's. Ruth kept telling me she liked me very much, but she was not ready for a permanent relationship. I am sure anyone else would have walked away. The more Ruth rejected me, the more I fought it. It wasn't just that I was infatuated with her, but a combination of things. She came from a middle-class family and was well educated. She seemed to have everything I had missed out on in life and I wanted to be part of it. I could see no wrong in what I was doing. I could not accept the thought of being cast aside. I probably needed professional help and didn't realise it at the time. The life I had led affected my judgement. I would think, "What's wrong with me? I don't drink or smoke. I am above average in most sports and in time Ruth will learn to love me." I thought the more I cared for her, the sooner she would love me. I never had much money, but whatever I had, I spent on Ruth, just to impress her. It was well known in town that the school teacher was George's girl. It never gave Ruth a chance to lead a normal social life. I guess over the twelve months since we first met, I wore her down, to the stage where she seemed happy enough to accept me as her permanent partner. In a couple of weeks, the school holidays would soon be here and Ruth was going home for Christmas. The thought of not being with Ruth played heavily on my mind and I decided to go to Melbourne, too. When Ruth found out about my intentions, she asked her parents if I could stay at their place by the seaside for the Christmas holidays. It was all arranged. I would go when I finished work and for the following three weeks, I managed to save a little money.

HOLIDAYS

*

I arrived at Ruth's place on Christmas Eve. More than nervous, I was scared. I stood outside this lovely home with its neatly trimmed lawns. Two large hydrangeas in full bloom covered part of the bedroom window. For several seconds, I wondered how I was going to pluck up enough courage to knock on the front door. During all this time, Ruth and her two sisters had been watching me through the window and probably wondering why I was just standing there. My concentration was broken by a rattle on the windowpane. I looked up and there was Ruth. Her two sisters, partly hidden by the hydrangeas, were laughing at my shyness.

Ruth came out to meet me. I followed her into the house where her parents were waiting in the lounge room to meet me. They must have thought I was a goose, as I kept blushing every time Ruth's father asked me a question. For the following two weeks, I was treated as one of the family. My shyness never left me, but when I was with Ruth, I was my old self. Ruth would say to me, "My family won't eat you." I did not impress anyone with my silence and I think Ruth's parents were glad to see me go back to the country so they could have Ruth on her own for the rest of the holidays. Before I said goodbye to Ruth and her family, I insisted on paying my way, but her mother wouldn't hear of it. I left five pounds on the piano with a thank you note. It was my way of expressing my feelings for not being rejected. Ruth still had three weeks left of her holidays and I was a lost soul, just waiting for her to return. I phoned her twice and each time her mother said Ruth was not home. I was worried something was wrong. The school holidays were nearly over and I had not been in touch with Ruth except for her one brief letter. Ruth was due back in a couple of days and I plucked up enough courage to ring her once more, but I got the same reply, "Ruth is out with her sisters."

IT'S OVER

*

I thought to myself, "Tomorrow Ruth will have to start school. She will come on the train late at night." I had no transport to go and meet her at the station, which was over twenty miles away, but I knew Ruth would catch the bus back to our town. I decided to go and meet her at the bus stop. I waited all day for that moment. It was around ten thirty when I saw the headlights of the bus appear. My heart was pounding as the passengers alighted one by one. There was no sign of Ruth. I didn't know what to think. I was looking for an excuse. "Maybe she had missed the train." I convinced myself that was what had happened and went back to the boarding house.

I didn't sleep at all. I twisted and turned most of the night, thinking about Ruth. It was in the early hours of the morning when I finally dozed off. I woke up feeling like a wet blanket. I couldn't eat my breakfast; my stomach was all churned up thinking about Ruth.

It was lunchtime when the phone rang at the factory. It was Ruth. Our conversation was short and cold. She wanted to meet after work at our favourite place by the river. For the rest of the day, my thoughts were not on my work. Ruth was going to break it off with me. I was waiting by the river bank when I saw Ruth pedaling her bike down the track towards me. She pulled up sharply and dropped her bike on the grass.

I knew by the look on her face it was over. Ruth used her parents as an excuse for breaking it off. She said they thought I was a nice person but we were both very young and should have a break from seeing each other for a while. I was devastated and lost for words. Unashamedly, tears ran down my face. Ruth stood there without saying a word. I managed to pull myself together and asked, "What happened last night? I waited to meet the bus." Ruth, still keeping her composure, not softening at my sadness and determined to finish our relationship said, "Mum and Dad drove me back yesterday morning and I arranged to board with a family I am friendly with. I didn't want to see you while Mum and Dad were here."

It didn't matter how much I tried to convince Ruth she was wrong; it was to no avail. I begged for us to stay together but Ruth came up with the same hurtful words, "I don't love you and I want my freedom." It was the end of everything I wanted in life. Ruth mounted her bike and rode away, her yellow and black spotted dress flapping over her knees as she disappeared down the grass track. I sat on the river bank until darkness, searching my soul for answers.

I think it was the first time in my life I failed to get what I wanted. For the next few weeks, I was a lost soul without Ruth. Several times I was tempted to ring her after she finished her classes. Ruth's words, that she wanted her freedom, rang in my ears day and night. When I came down for my meals, the boys sensed what I was going through and hardly a word was spoken at the table. The dining room was never the same again and I always felt alone, more so when I was eating my meal. Images of Ruth appeared across the table. I was torturing myself with these illusions. How many times had we sat together at this table and shared a meal in laughter? I couldn't stand this consistent reminder of Ruth and thought it best if I moved out of the boarding house.

THE TOWN BALL

*

I was offered a part-time job at one of the hotels in return for free board. As the weeks passed, I was starting to feel like my old self again. I had heard Ruth was dating a boy from another town. It didn't have much of an effect on me. I felt free and full of life again. I had become friendly with the daughter of the hotel owner and we were spending a lot of time together.

The annual Town Ball was coming up soon. It was the most important event of the year and I decided to take my new girlfriend to there. I thought if Ruth was there with her friend, I could show her there was more than one attractive woman in town who was interested in me. I was surprised to see Ruth with a group of elderly people from the church where she took drama classes after school and soon realised the new Minister had escorted her to the ball. We met during the Progressive Barn Dance. I didn't speak and pretended I was somewhere else as we danced. "That's a pretty girl you are with tonight," said Ruth as we parted. If she only knew how my heart was pounding as I held her in my arms. I didn't ask her to dance during the night. I kept making contact with her eyes as she danced around the hall. I had nearly forgotten I had a partner. She sensed I wasn't with her and that my mind was somewhere else. I was told in no uncertain manner that I had spoilt her night and not to bother to see her again.

TOGETHER AGAIN

*

Ruth rang two days later and said she wanted to see me at our favourite place after work. She realised when she saw me at the ball with someone else that she was wrong and wanted to be with me again. Ruth was there under the tree waiting for me when I arrived. We embraced and she said, "I wanted time to think about us after the holidays." I guess I felt just the same as Ruth. I was just happy to have her back. I felt on top of the world when I left her a little while later and we had decided to go to the pictures that night. It was like our first date as we rode our bikes over the bridge. Our bikes were our transport; if one of the bikes had a flat tyre, I would dink Ruth to wherever we were going. Our relationship over the next several months was running a lot smoother since our break up, so much that Ruth now fully accepted our relationship and broke the news to her parents about us. Soon it would be Christmas once again; I was surer of myself when I arrived at her parents' place this time. I greeted her mother with an affectionate hug and her father shook my hand as if he was glad to see me again. I was more relaxed with this meeting and lost most of my shyness at the dinner table. During my previous visit, I had dreaded meal time and hardly ate anything. I felt all eyes were on me with every mouthful I took.

During the following three weeks, Ruth and I spent our time idling our hours away on the sandy beach with Ruth's sister and her boyfriend, who taught at the same school. We had nothing in common. All day he had his head buried in a book. I was surrounded by teachers and found myself completely out of my depth.

My past life was my secret. Even Ruth knew very little about it. I was too ashamed to talk about my Dad. I was sure Ruth's parents would have rejected me. Not everyone one is born with the right parents.

WEDDING BELLS

*

One Saturday night, Ruth and I went to a dance with her sister and her sister's boyfriend. The band was playing The Tennessee Waltz. I was in another world with Ruth in my arms when it popped out, "I think we should get married." Ruth said yes, but we would have to ask her parents first. The following day, I kept putting off speaking to her father; just waiting for the right moment. It was towards evening and Ruth's father was in the backyard watering the garden when I saw my chance to speak to him. For a moment he didn't speak; I think he was in a state of shock. He looked at me and his first words were, "I had better break the news to Mum." Ruth had joined me and we waited in the garden for their answer.

Both her parents appeared on the back verandah with big smiles on their faces. Ruth said, "It's all right," and I was given an affectionate hug by her mother. We then all went inside and toasted our future with champagne. Ruth was their eldest daughter and I felt while we were drinking champagne, Ruth's parents' faces showed disappointment that their daughter hadn't made a better choice. Maybe in their minds, my future was limited.

My holidays were coming to an end. In the two years we'd been together, never was there any attempt to go further than a kiss or a cuddle. But things changed after we got engaged and within the last week of my holidays, we made love for the first time. The next day, it was time for me to leave Ruth and return home to start work. Ruth still had three weeks of her holidays left before school started.

I was now engaged and with very little money. I made every effort to save enough money to buy an engagement ring, then the unexpected happened. A few weeks after Ruth returned from her holidays, she rang me after school, saying she wanted to see me. She said, "Don't worry. I will see you at our meeting place." I wasn't a bit worried about our relationship, but I did wonder why she wanted to see me. Ruth said she was pregnant. What was I going to do? I had no idea at this moment. Her parents insisted we get married within the next six weeks. Ruth never asked me if I had any money; I was stony broke. All my money had gone in pleasing Ruth over the past two years. For the past three weeks, I had just managed to save enough money to buy the engagement ring. I guess I was like my Dad in some ways, "Tomorrow will look after its self."

There was not much time left before the six weeks were up for our wedding. I was better than average at Kelly pool and managed to win a few pounds at the local billiard room. I saved twelve pounds; that's all I had to my name. I made arrangements to be married on Saturday night at seven o'clock. Ruth's parents arrived on the Friday, the day before the wedding and booked into the best hotel in the town. It was arranged we would have dinner at the same hotel.

For the last couple of days, I had been undecided if I should take a risk. A good friend of mine had a greyhound racing at the local greyhound track on the Friday night, a day before the wedding. He was fairly confident his dog could win if the favourite missed the start. I thought, "What can I do with twelve pounds? If I back the dog and it wins, my troubles will be over for a few days. I was sitting at the dining room table with Ruth and her parents. All my thoughts were on whether I should leave the table and put my twelve pounds on the dog. More than once Ruth asked me if there was something wrong. I kept looking at my watch; the race would be on in half an hour. Suddenly, I stood up and said, "I have something to do." Leaving my unfinished meal, I ran all the way to the dog track in a few minutes. It was a hurdle race. Gay Scotch, the favourite from box one, was odds on. My friend's dog, Command, was second favourite at six to one. Clutching the twelve pounds, I walked over to where Ron was parading his greyhound. He stopped for a moment and asked what price his dog was. "Six to one," I said. Ron then gave me twenty pounds to put on his dog. That's all the confidence I needed to put my twelve pounds on.

I was now stony broke. The race was ready to start. The greyhounds were in the starting boxes. Any moment the lids would fly open and release the greyhounds. My eyes were firmly fixed on the number one box, hoping the favourite would miss the start. To my dismay, the favourite jumped three lengths clear of the field. It was all over bar the shouting. The favourite was now ten lengths in front of Ron's dog coming to the second last hurdle. Then the unexpected happened. Instead of jumping the last hurdle, the favourite followed the lure through the trap door beside it. Gay Scott was disqualified for not jumping the last hurdle. Ron's dog was awarded the race for coming second. I could not believe what had happened. Eighty-four pounds in my pocket! Walking back to the hotel, I thought, "Someone is looking after me." It was about nine o'clock when I arrived back at the hotel. The dining room table was deserted and Ruth and her parents were sitting in the lounge room waiting for me. While I was at the greyhound meeting, my future in-laws had decided what we would do tomorrow. It was decided Ruth would spend the day with her mother and I would have lunch with Ruth's father and have a talk about our future. I said, "I am playing my last game of football tomorrow." For a moment there was silence; you could have heard a pin drop. Ruth's parents must have thought, "What in the heck does our daughter see in this bloke?"

After a while, Ruth's parents had had enough and decided to retire to their rooms. I had never told anyone I was getting married, not even my brother, or asked him for money. I was very much like my Dad. What you don't have today, you will have tomorrow. By the time the football bus arrived back from Albury, I barely had enough time to be at the church by seven o'clock. When I arrived with my one and only suitcase, dressed in a new suit I'd managed to buy a couple of weeks before the wedding, Ruth's parents were waiting at the front door of the Church of England with Ruth. For a brief moment, there was a slight delay; we didn't have a witness. Fortunately, the Minster's son was at the Manse and came to our aid. Half an hour later, we were married and on our way to Albury with Ruth's parents, who had booked us all into a hotel for the night. Looking back over the years, I wonder how many newlyweds have their in-laws with them on their wedding night. The next morning, Ruth's parents returned to Melbourne, none the wiser about our plans for the future. We spent Sunday looking around Albury and had lunch in the gardens. At night, we decided to go to church.

Sitting in the lounge room of the hotel after church I thought, "It must be very expensive to stay here. On the Monday morning, I decided to check out the price of staying there. Thirty-three pounds. I paid the account. It was now time to front Ruth and tell her I had no savings, except for forty-seventy pounds. Ruth didn't get upset. She said, "I have forty-five pounds in the bank." We sat on the bed and for the first time we talked about what we should do. Ruth suggested we had enough money to go to Sydney and find work. I wasn't keen on going to Sydney. I thought Melbourne was a better place to find a job. So, it was decided we would look for a cheap flat to rent.

Arriving in Melbourne, we stayed at a hotel for two days while we tried to find a place to live. We never had a chance to rent; every time we found a flat, the agent wanted key money. We were now in a hopeless position, with very little money. Ruth decided to ring her parents. Ruth's mother answered the phone and was happy for a brief moment. "Where are you ringing from?" Ruth answered, "We are in Melbourne and have nowhere to live." There was silence, then Ruth's father came on the phone. It was decided we come straight to their place. The next morning at breakfast, my mother-in-law started to lay down the law to me in a very heavy manner, just as I'd sometimes heard her speaking to her husband. Even though I was at their mercy, I wouldn't take any of this talk and walked out of the house. For the next week, I was back in my old world. I went and found my father and stayed with him. We went bottleoing most days; it was just like old times. I didn't tell Dad I was married. But I was missing Ruth, so on the Sunday morning I rang her. She wanted me to come back, saying, "Everything will be alright." That was the one and only time I had cross words with my mother-in-law.

LOOKING AHEAD

*

I soon found work with a plaster firm and was surprised when I got my first pay packet, fifteen pounds. My brother had only been paying me eight pounds a week for the same work. For the past four and a half years, my brother had been underpaying me. No wonder I was always struggling for money. In my new job, I had to leave Chelsea at five-thirty in the morning and arrived home around seven at night in the dark, which meant I saw very little of Ruth. My father-in-law had a first class set of carpentry tools and I was allowed to use them, providing I took great care. My early jobs in the furniture trade were a blessing. I made all the furniture for the nursery before the baby was born. I surprised my father-in-law. During his whole life, he had just sat behind a desk. He loved nothing better than to spend time with me in the shed. As the years passed, we became the best of mates.

A BABY GIRL

*

It was about seven o'clock in the evening when Ruth got her first sign that things were starting to happen. She was in labour for several hours at the Chelsea Hospital and suffered a great deal of pain before the baby arrived. The next morning, before I went to work, I visited Ruth. She looked as if she had just woken up from a lovely sleep. I badly wanted a boy and when I heard it was a girl, I wanted to bury my head in the sand. The last thing I wanted was a girl. My experiences of rejection were working against the opposite sex. Was it because my mother left me when I was a five-week-old baby? I didn't nurse my daughter very much and I did not ever change her nappy. We had no thoughts of having another child, but with little protection, Ruth became pregnant again.

MY FIRST CONTRACT

*

During the past year, I had been learning the fixing side of plastering. I was given the chance by my firm and they were not too happy when I told them I was leaving and going to work for myself. I tendered for my first plastering job and was successful. My contract price was six hundred and forty pounds and after paying all expenses, I made two hundred and seventy pounds for five days' work. I was following the tenders in The Age for work. A firm on the other side of Melbourne was looking for a subcontract plasterer. I decided to take the job as I could make good money. It was a long day travelling from Chelsea to Greensborough, but it was well worth the effort as I was making sixty pounds a week. The average wage was around twenty-five pounds. I also worked in the plaster factory at weekends, making plaster cornices on contract and on Saturday nights I would sleep on the couch in the lunchroom to save the travelling on Sundays.

A NEW LESSON

*

I was working towards the goal of owning our own home. It all came to a sudden end when the owner of the plaster works went broke. I was owed eight hundred pounds for my past work and had not been paid. The only way I thought I could retrieve my money was to take over the plaster factory with what little stock was left. The rent was fifteen pounds a week and there were several unhappy builders waiting for their plaster to be finished, which I was not responsible for. We rented a house for two pounds a week and moved closer to my work. This venture proved to be a total disaster. Within twelve months, I lost everything I worked for. After paying off my workers, I closed the factory, three days before Christmas, with just five shillings left in my pocket to buy whatever for Christmas.

The next morning, I bought The Age and searched the tenders for any plastering jobs. There was only one plastering job advertised, three rooms to be plastered in St Kilda. Desperate for money, I tendered a low price of seventy-five pounds. At eleven o'clock on the Friday morning, a day before Christmas day, I finished the job and with fifty pounds in my pocket, my worries were over until I found work. The business owed nineteen hundred pounds to various firms and I made arrangements to pay all the money I owed them. It wasn't the lack of hard work that lost me my business; it was lack of an education and the knowledge that book-keeping was the key to running a successful business. When I first started my own business, my father-in-law, who was an accountant, offered to take care of the books for me, but I refused.

After the Christmas holidays, I managed to get a large contracting job in Surrey Hills. It was an estate of one hundred and twenty houses. For the next fourteen months, I employed a plasterer and a labourer to help me. I worked six days a week and paid back all the money I owed. I also managed to buy a block of land next door to where we were living. Every day after work, I'd scrounge around the estate for leftover materials to build a part of my first home. Ruth was expecting our fourth child, which was a big mistake. We'd only wanted three children. I was now doing quite well with my work and even found time to play cricket and my favourite sporting game, table tennis. I had just won the Diamond Valley single and doubles tournaments and was now taking lessons from the Australian table tennis coach to try and improve my defence, which was a weakness in my game.

FATE

*

Fate was to take me in another direction. My brother appeared on my doorstep and wanted to sell his plaster works to me for seven hundred pounds. It was a bargain, I thought. This is where my upbringing led me to make a bad judgement without thinking of the consequences. Within one week, I had finished closing down all my contracts and was back in the same country town, reliving the youth that I had once fled. My brother had not been honest about the plaster works. He had no orders for work and had lost most of his builders; gambling had at last caught up with him. The factory was depleted. Unbeknown to me, there was a Bill of Sale of four hundred pounds owing to the bank and within one day of my arrival, my brother's former bank manager paid me a visit at the factory. He was demanding the money be paid back or the factory would stay closed. The manager knew he had lent the money against very little security and he was desperate to make a deal. I came to an arrangement with him. I would give him the title to my half house in Melbourne, take responsibility for the Bill of Sale, and obtain a thousand-pound overdraft. The owner of the factory insisted I pay the back rent of one hundred and sixty pounds or I could not rent the factory at two pounds a week. I paid my brother the balance of the money. He kept insisting he didn't owe the bank or factory rent any money. The factory was so run down. Its doors had been closed for several weeks. It had a bad reputation and when this happens in a small town, it's nearly impossible to start again. Slowly I managed to get a little work, through begging and promising the builders I could do a good job. The word soon spread around the town that my work was first class and the builders returned one by one. There wasn't as much work in the area as when I was there before. Things had changed a lot in the seven years I had been away. I had imagined it would be the same when I returned but was now looking for any sort of income to support the factory.

TWO VAGABONDS

*

I saw an opportunity to make a little money. The local billiard room was closed and for sale. I bought it for one hundred and fifty pounds. The Murray River flowed close to the town. Two swaggies lived on the river bank in their tin hut, a couple of hundred yards from the bridge. I often stopped and talked to them in the main street and said they could come up at night and sit in the billiard room. Soon they were doing little jobs in the rooms. I trusted these two old men and let them look after the billiard room for me during week nights. The billiard tables were brushed every day and the place was kept spotless. There was a shower for them in the back room and they could make themselves a cup of tea. On winter nights, the two of them never missed coming up to the rooms to sit around the open log fire and take care of things for me. The next day they handed over the takings and never once did I have any worries that they'd cheated me. The town folk looked down on these two swaggies as hopeless vagabonds. My childhood experience with these men allowed them into my heart. I was now doing better financially with the two businesses. I still needed something else if I was to get ahead. The local bottle yard was on the market for eight hundred pounds. I bought the brewery license for eight hundred pounds and was doing very well with the new business. My wife didn't like me collecting beer bottles. It caused so much trouble between us that I had to sell the license back at half what I bought it for. This cost me a nice income and I lost money.

THE FIRE

*

One Sunday evening, we were all sitting around the dinner table when the fire siren sounded. The children wanted to see the fire, so we all made a rush for the car and followed the fire truck down the main street. To my surprise, the billiard room was ablaze. It was totally destroyed and with it, I had lost my second income within a matter of weeks. Even though it was insured for five hundred pounds, I was now finding it hard to make ends meet. There was a slump in the building trade and my overdraft was at its limit. I had to do something quickly. I decided to put the plaster works on the market and move back to Melbourne as soon as possible. I found a buyer if I financed the deal. I sold it for two thousand pounds, on two hundred pounds deposit, plus monthly payments. We had been living here for nearly four years. With all my ups and downs, we managed to build a new house, but now it was impossible to sell before we moved back to Melbourne. While I made all these decisions, whether to our advantage or not, Ruth never interfered, except for the bottle yard. I had enough and seemed to be getting nowhere and decided to move back to Melbourne.

RETURN TO MELBOURNE

*

Within two days of arriving back, I found a contracting job and I was now in full flight, working long hours seven days a week. One night, driving home from work, I saw a large supermarket under construction. I made enquiries about the plastering. If I could meet their price, the job was mine. I sat down and did my homework and for the next five years I worked full-time plastering for this firm.

I was now financial enough to buy a house in Noble Park, a plain L- shaped weatherboard. A little later, we were in the position to buy a second brick house in Sandown Park. The children were starting to be a little independent. Ruth decided to go back to teaching. It gave her back the life she had missed.

DEATH OF A BOTTLEO

*

My father was unable to work. His hard life and drinking had finally caught up with him. For the past two years, I had been paying the rent for his house, the light bill and the gas to make things a little easier for him in his old age. There were four of them, my Dad, his woman Violet, and his two mates Mocka and Ossie, living in a single-fronted terrace house in North Melbourne. Now a lifetime had slipped by. Quite often in the past, they had shared each other's roof when in need. Now the time had come when they all needed each other. They didn't have much; worldly possessions meant very little to them. A bed and a bottle of beer were more than enough. They shared what little they had; just living together and living from one pension day to the next. Their loyalty and companionship eliminated all loneliness. They had what others didn't have, comradeship. Only time could take it away from them.

My Dad "King Bob" was the boss. He gave the orders and organised the pension money. Whatever he said was never questioned. They all knew while King Bob was alive, there would be a roof over their heads and a warm bed to sleep in. It was not necessary for them to be reminded what it was like, on a winter's night, to sleep on a park bench with only a newspaper covering them to stop them freezing to death.

Ossie worshipped King Bob. Whenever there was an errand to be done, Ossie was there. It wouldn't matter what he had to do, his answer was always the same, "Yes Bob, you're the boss." As a young man, Ossie was like any other youth. He came from a good family background and had a bright future until he fell victim to the drink. Now the only thing he had left in the world was King Bob and his two friends.

My Dad and Violet seldom raised their voices to each other and the days of waking up with black eyes and abuse had long gone. Violet had once been a beautiful woman. As a young starlet in the 1930s, she had danced and sang at vaudeville shows, performing in the suburbs of Melbourne. She had also danced in the chorus at the old Tivoli Theatre. My father picked her up one afternoon at the local hotel in Napier Street, Fitzroy, so many years ago he couldn't remember when. She was an alcoholic and the hard life had left its mark on her. Yet when she smiled, a touch of beauty enhanced her face and your thoughts would soften towards her. Now she was content to spend the twilight of her life in bed with King Bob. Her most prized possession was her scrap book, partly buried in the grubby bed covers, only to be retrieved when an unexpected caller came. A piece of broken magnifying glass would be held unsteadily in her hand, while she would affectively turn each page. Her face would look for approval, as if it was her final curtain call.

The other member of the unbreakable team was Mocka, Bob's best mate. Mocka was once a prize fighter but had never made the main event. He was not a pretty sight. I would visit my Dad a few days before pension day to see if they had enough food and drink. Three days can seem like a long time waiting for the pension. My Dad would joke with Mocka, "Show Jumbo how you fought those twelve-rounders." For a brief moment Mocka would relive the past, throwing punches at an imaginary opponent. "Did you see that, Jumbo? I got him with my left hook. You know Bob, if it wasn't for the booze, I could have been a champion!" His slurred speech and cauliflower ear told other stories.

One bottle of wine was Mocka's ration for the day. Every day King Bob would fill a small flask from a bottle of wine and keep it until it was time for Mocha to go to bed. Each night, Mocka would cuddle it like a baby and sip away till the bottle was empty. He knew the rules and would never press Bob for more wine. He would just sit around the next day and wait for King Bob to hand out his ration.

The front room of the single-fronted house was their kingdom. Hidden from the outside world, it was here King Bob and his woman spent most of their time in bed, except for pension day. The four of them would make the journey to the post office to collect their pensions. All the money was handed over to their leader. They knew they would have one long week of drinking when Bob took care of the money. There were no bills to pay. The rent was paid and the electric light was not a necessity in their mind; King Bob preferred to have the money for a drink instead of me paying a light bill. They were quite content with the hurricane lamp hanging from the light cord. King Bob would decide how much beer they would drink each day and sometimes the money would last until the middle of the second week. When all the money was gone, they would wait for me to arrive. If I didn't make it on that day, my Dad would send Mocka and Ossie out with the pram to collect empty beer bottles around the streets of North Melbourne, to get money for a much-needed drink. On a winter's night, Mocka and Ossie loved to sit around the open fireplace on their wooden boxes, tenderly feeding the fire with pieces of wood they had collected from the disposable rubbish bins. Ossie would carefully watch the blackened billy come to the boil, waiting for the right moment to dispose of the tea tightly clutched in his hand. Ossie knew if he messed it up, the tea leaves would settle on top and all the tapping on the side of the billy would not settle them. When this happened, Bob would abuse and swear at him. If his rage continued, he would send Ossie off to bed like a little child. It was the same with Mocka. He would be sitting on his box next to Ossie, watching the dripping in the cast iron frying pan so it wouldn't catch alight and burn the fried bread or the sizzling sausages. This would all be washed down with billy tea.

From his bed, King Bob would give the orders as they washed the few dishes in a dented enamel dish which hung from a bent nail on the back of the front door, next to a tea towel which had long ago lost its identity. As long as everything served a purpose and they didn't have to move out of the room, pride was a thing of the past. If there was ever a little spare money, King Bob would send Mocka to the hardware store to buy several hanks of string and some brass rings. Mocka and Ossie would sit on their wooden boxes by the fireplace, with a half-made rabbit net hanging on a nail from the fire surround. They would work away with a wooden needle wrapped in rabbit string. After making two or three dozen nets, Ossie would take the nets over to Collingwood, to a buyer who ran a small business. It was their way of making a little extra money. My Dad loved nothing better than to talk about his past deals on the bottle cart when I made my usual visit just before pension day to see that everything was alright. Dad liked to be the centre of attention when I went to visit him. He would always spin a good yarn for my sake about one of his deals. The older he got, the bigger the deals became. "Remember the time Mocka, we were drinking at the Peel Hotel. Ossie boasted he was a better dealer than me. I told him to get the horse and cart and we would work Gipps Street. We took one side each of Gipps Street and whoever had the most scrap by the time we reached the end of the street, won the bet. I was doing alright, picking up metal and two bags of rags. You Ossie were loading the cart with bath heaters, coppers and a bike. I couldn't work out how you could pull so much stuff in one street until this woman came screaming out of the house saying a thief had taken her copper. You bastard, you threw her washing on the ground to get to the copper. You were lucky not to finish in the lockup for the night. She turned out to be a good sport after I spent the night with her." Violet didn't bat an eyelid; she knew King Bob had a weakness for stray women. Over the years, more than once, she shared her bed with another woman.

King Bob didn't like warm beer and there was no electricity, so he set up a bottle cooler in the laundry trough. It was simple, but effective. My Dad placed a small wooden box in the laundry trough and covered it with a hessian bag. By letting the water drip, it soon wet the hessian bag and kept the beer cool. It was so effective you could freeze a pound of butter. There was not a thing to worry about while King Bob was alive. King Bob and his woman seldom left the bed these days; even on pension day it was an effort for them. Dad knew he was getting weaker and his days were numbered. In his weak voice, he would talk about heading back to the bush and finding a nice little place to live in. "You know Mocka, we could live in the tin hut where Jumbo and I spent the winter once, until we found a place. First, we will have to get some money together and make a lot of rabbit nets, then we will all head for the bush."

It was only memories of the past talking. The drink always came first. Finally, it took its toll on my Dad. One morning he woke up and said, "I don't feel very well, get me Jumbo." My phone number was written in bold red letters across the smoke- stained chimney breast. It read, "Ring Jumbo if Dad's sick." My phone number hung silently; it didn't exist in their demented minds.

Somehow my Dad was admitted to the Royal Melbourne Hospital. Fate had dealt me a hard blow. I hadn't seen my Dad for two weeks as I had been on holidays with my family and as we returned on the Monday, I drove down Flemington Road and passed the Royal Melbourne Hospital. I casually remarked to my wife I should turn off at the next intersection and see how Dad was. Ruth was tired from the long trip and wanted to go home. It didn't take much persuasion to put it out of my mind for the time being. Unbeknown to me, my Dad had lain in hospital for three days and the only words he uttered were, "Get me Jumbo." It was his will to see me that made him hang on to life a little longer. My phone number hung in silence. What meaning did it have to three derelicts who had lost all sense of communication. I was one day late. Two days before pension day, I arrived with the usual supplies. The moment

I walked through the door, I knew something was wrong. The three of them were like lost souls, Violet sitting up in bed, Ossie and Mocka sitting around the blackened fireplace. I noticed there was no firewood. Mocka mumbled something about the hospital and the funeral parlour. I couldn't get any sense out of them. They were lost without their leader. I went straight to the hospital and was fortunate to meet the doctor who had treated my dad. Our conversation was short. He just said my Dad had died while waiting for me and arrangements had been made with Tobin Brothers in Flemington Road for the funeral. I thanked the doctor and made my way to Tobin Brothers to clear up this confusion. I made enquiries about my Dad and was told there was no one by that name. I decided to go back to the house to see what they had done with Dad. This time I was really mad with them. They muttered something about going to the funeral place around the corner. I went straight back to Tobin Brothers to sort out the mess. I made enquiries again and discovered they had a funeral the next day for a Mr. Burns. I asked the receptionist if I could have a look at the casket as I was sure Mr. Burns was my Dad. It was against their policy, but in cases like these, they allowed it. I got quite a shock. My Dad was like a little doll. He looked so peaceful. It was like the way he lived; he never worried about tomorrow. As he would say, "It will take care of itself." At last it was all sorted out and I rearranged the funeral for the following Monday. It had been Violet's idea to give a false name and address because they had no money to pay for a funeral. She wanted King Bob to have a decent funeral. On the day of the funeral, my Uncle George arrived, much to my surprise. He had not spoken a word to his brother for a number of years. Why on earth he came to the funeral, I don't know. The sight of him brought unpleasant memories back to me of when I was a child, and I wanted revenge.

The service was attended by Dad's derelict friends who roamed the streets close by. In Dad's eyes, I was his only son and he would have been pleased if he knew I was there to say goodbye to him. I specially made arrangements for a coach car so my Dad's mates could pay their last respects. When the coach arrived outside the funeral parlour, my Uncle George made a dash for the back seat, much to my anger. To get even, I piled two derelicts in the back seat each side of my uncle just to embarrass him. He was locked in the middle of the back-car seat. It gave me great satisfaction to see the look on his face as he tried to get out of the car. My Dad would have been proud of me. Three weeks after the funeral, I went back to the house and found everyone had left. I closed everything down and the only thing I took was Dad's crib board. Whatever happened to Violet, I never tried to find out. I feel sure after Dad passed away,

Violet would not have had the will to live. Without Dad to give them guidance and support, Mocka and Ossie drifted back to the gardens and parks that were to become their home once again. In time, I returned to Fitzroy and wandered through the garden paths looking for my Dad's mates. They were in their usual place, hiding behind a bed of native shrubs, like a pair of lost souls. Their faces lit up as I approached them. We would reminisce for a few minutes about Dad. When a lone tear appeared on Ossie's cheek, his mate would pass him the bottle, wrapped in a brown paper bag, to ease the pain. The warmth of an open fireplace, watching the billy boil, with King Bob looking over them, was now only a memory. Sleeping in the gardens on a park bench, covered in newspapers on a winter's night, was now their home. Ossie died that coming winter. I still made an occasional visit to the gardens to see Mocka .He'd be sitting on a park bench with a new found mate, passing their bottle back and forth, until time caught up with him. There was no need to visit the park anymore; only the memory of them sitting around the open fireplace, idolising their King, remains with me now.

TIME PASSES BY

*

As the years passed by, Ruth and I slowly drifted apart. I think being rejected as a child made me think I was not capable of being loved. My wife and family, in certain ways, suffered. I believe it is an illness that needs treatment at an early stage of life. It was not till later in life I tried to understand how to handle rejection.

MEMORIES NEVER FADE

*

After we divorced, I'd frequently come back to Fitzroy and think of the good times I had shared with my Dad. I returned to my birthplace to retrace my childhood memories, walking around the streets and the back lanes of Fitzroy, occasionally stopping outside a two-storey house and looking up at the balcony window. My thoughts were full of memories of how Dad and I lived in that room and many other rooms or dilapidated houses, around Fitzroy and Collingwood. I would stop and give all my thoughts to where a row of terraced houses once stood. Now a modern factory, with glass walls reflecting the sunlight, stands where Dad and I once pulled many a bottle.

His idea of a good education was the bottle cart. I can see him now, standing beside the bottle cart in his bib and brace overalls, his toothless grin lighting up his face, "That was a good deal, Jumbo. You will never be short of a shilling if you know how to do a good deal." My Dad taught me what all the education in the world could never do - how to survive in life without depending on others. I found myself standing outside the house where I was born. A large, gaping crack ran down the face of the brickwork, the layers of peeling paint a reminder of the past. Two young boys were playing a game of marbles on the same patch of ground that I did as a boy. Did they live in this house? Did they sleep in the room where I was born? I pressed my face up against a window pane, trying to get a glimpse inside the room where I was born. I must have disturbed someone, for I was startled by a heavy voice, "What in the hell are you doing?" Before I could look around, two burly men grabbed me. I was forced against the house wall. They called me foul names and I received a nasty punch in the ribs. The pain was excruciating as I tried to turn around but was held hard against the wall. Then they released their grip on me slightly. It was enough for me to turn around and face them. I tried to tell them that I'd been born in this house and explained what I was doing there. They seemed to understand a little but told me to piss off. The two young kids were now more interested in my plight than their marbles. After such a scare, I took a stroll along Brunswick Street and retraced another part of my early life. I soon found my way to Mario's Café and ordered a cup of coffee. From my table I saw a twenty-dollar note passed over the counter, with little thought to what the change might be. It made me think of the time when this cafe was a fish and chip shop, ready to feed many a hungry mouth. As a young boy, I once stood six deep at the counter, holding a penny high above my head, hoping to be noticed. My hungry eyes fixed firmly on a basket of chips, hoping the man with the sweaty forehead might shake a few extra chips for me onto the bundle of newspapers neatly piled on the counter. White paper was seldom used in those early days to protect the fish and chips from the newspaper. I was drifting into another time zone. Two young people were oblivious to me as I brushed past a table. Their searching eyes told another story.

WHY I ASKED MYSELF

*

Standing outside Mario's, I decided to make my way to the Rob Roy Hotel. Old habits never die. I sat down on the front step like when I was a child, waiting for the hotel to close so I could take my Dad home. My memories were strong as I walked towards Johnson Street. I paused for a moment and thought of Jimmy "The Duke" and his hansom cab, parked outside the post office on a Saturday morning, waiting to take his regulars to the Flemington races for one and sixpence a head. Before I caught a train back to my unit, I wanted to see my Grandma's house again. It was only a few minutes' walk to Gore Street. Standing outside the house, memories came flooding back, how one knock on my Grandma's front door changed my life forever, for better or worse only I can judge that.

ACKNOWLEDGEMENTS

Grateful thanks to my first wife Ruth who helped me so much with my English, both spoken and written, when we first married and to my second wife Marlene who I met when I was 79 and has been a power of strength to me as we worked together checking and correcting my book so that it is now being published nearly 30 years after it was written.

ABOUT THE AUTHOR

George began writing quite late in life. His first story, 'My Dad', was published in a book of short stories, 'The Man Who Played Spoons'. His second story, 'Looking Back', won first prize in a competition run by the city of Casey. In 1989, Ros Bowman interviewed him about his unusual childhood for her programme, 'Word of Mouth' on the ABC radio. This attracted so much interest from listeners that they did a second interview. Sometime later, he wrote a book about his early life, but then lost interest in writing and only now, at 90, with time running out, has decided to publish it.

Shawline Publishing Group Pty Ltd
www.shawlinepublishing.com.au

CPSIA information can be obtained
at www.ICGtesting.com
Printed in the USA
LVHW101908090222
710699LV00019B/662

9 781922 594990